Piano Solo

THE WORLD'S GREAT CLASS[

Piano Classics

40 Original Works by 22 Composers

Intermediate to Advanced Piano Solos

EDITED BY MARGARET OTWELL AND RICHARD WALTERS

MARK CARLSTEIN, ASSISTANT EDITOR

ISBN 978-0-634-01265-5

HAL•LEONARD®
CORPORATION

7777 W. BLUEMOUND RD. P.O. BOX 13819 MILWAUKEE, WI 53213

Visit Hal Leonard Online at
www.halleonard.com

CONTENTS

ABOUT THE COMPOSERS...

JOHANN SEBASTIAN BACH (1685-1750).

Johann Sebastian Bach's incomparable genius for musical form and structure is revered more than 300 years after his birth. Yet the Baroque master and his music were actually forgotten by the general public and musicians alike for many years. Musical fashions were already changing by Bach's later years, and his music was heard less frequently than earlier in his lifetime. After his death, which may have been hastened by treatments and surgery for blindness, his music fell out of fashion. His second wife, Anna Magdelena, died in poverty about ten years later. Bach's works span a wide range of genres. He wrote liturgical works, Lutheran masses, church and secular cantatas, chamber music, organ works, orchestral pieces, concertos, vocal and choral pieces as well as compositions for clavier. In his day he was widely known as a virtuoso organist. His improvisational skills were legendary. With his contemporary George Frideric Handel, whom he never met, he was one of the last great composers of the Baroque era. Some ninety years after Bach's death, his works were once again brought before the public by the composer and conductor Felix Mendelssohn. Mendelssohn became a champion of the works of Bach and other composers who had been pushed aside with the shifting of musical fashions. Bach's music has been a mainstay of the international repertoire ever since.

BÉLA BARTÓK (1881-1945).

Known both as a composer and a pianist, Béla Bartók made an indelible mark on the classical music world though his interest in folk music, particularly that of his native Hungary. With composer Zoltan Kodály, Bartok carefully researched and transcribed great quantities of folk music; their studies took them to the most remote corners of the country. Both composers used these melodies in their own compositions. Bartók stopped composing for a time to devote himself to the collection and study of the folk music of various other cultures. As a young man Bartók attended the Budapest Academy, soon earning a reputation for composing dissonant, somewhat violent music. By middle age his style mellowed to more subtle, delicate sounds. During the 1930s the composer became harshly critical of the fascist regimes in Europe, prohibiting performances of his music in Italy and Germany and arranging to have his papers and manuscripts moved to London for safety. In the final months of 1940, following the death of his mother, Bartók fled the war in Europe and moved to New York City. He found life in New York a difficult adjustment and struggled to support himself. Eventually he received a grant to research a collection of Slavic folk music at Harvard. His health began to deteriorate, forcing him to rely on the American Society of Composers, Authors and Publishers (ASCAP) for assistance with medical costs. He died in New York in 1945. It is said that shortly before he died he said to his doctor, "The trouble is that I have to go with much still to say."

LUDWIG VAN BEETHOVEN (1770-1827).

It is difficult to know how much of our perception of Beethoven is myth and how much is fact. He was the greatest composer of his era, certainly. Beethoven began his musical studies with his father, a Bonn court musician. He was appointed as deputy court organist in Bonn when he was eleven years old. He later continued his studies with Haydn, until differences between the two ended their relationship. Beethoven was first known to the public as a brilliant, flamboyant piano virtuoso, but there was a much darker aspect to his life. He was devastated when, in his late teens, he was summoned home from Vienna to keep vigil at his mother's deathbed. The second great tragedy of his life began when he was quite young, as a slight hearing impairment. Then in 1802, when the composer was 32, he was informed by doctors that he would eventually lose his hearing altogether. Beethoven sank into a deep despair, during which he wrote a will of sorts to his brothers. Whether or not he was considering suicide is a subject of some speculation. Whatever the case, the "Heiligenstadt Testament," as the will is known, states that he believed he would soon be dead. He eventually came to terms with his deafness and went on to write some of his most powerful pieces. His last six symphonies were written in the following years. In addition to his nine symphonies, Beethoven wrote pieces in nearly every imaginable genre. His works include an oratorio, two ballets, an opera, incidental music for various theatrical productions, military music, cantatas, a wealth of chamber music, 32 piano sonatas, various piano pieces, some 85 songs and 170 folksong arrangements. At Beethoven's funeral, on March 29, 1827, some 10,000 people joined in his funeral procession. One of the torch-bearers was composer Franz Schubert, who had idolized Beethoven. Some 45 years after his funeral, Beethoven's body was moved to Vienna's Central Cemetery, where he lies near the grave of Schubert.

JOHANNES BRAHMS (1833-1897).

Johannes Brahms was a man of strong opinions. He disapproved of the "New German School" of composers, namely Liszt and Wagner. He avoided what he believed to be the excesses of the tone poem, relying instead on traditional symphonic forms. After his Symphony No. 1 was premiered, he was hailed as "Beethoven's true heir." The symphony, written when Brahms was forty-three years old, is so clearly linked to the symphonies of Beethoven that it has jokingly been called "Beethoven's Tenth." Brahms began his musical studies as a youngster, gaining experience in composition and working as an arranger for his father's light orchestra. He revered composer Robert Schumann. On the advice of Franz Liszt he met Schumann, with whom he developed a close friendship. He also developed a deep love for Schumann's wife, Clara Wieck Schumann. From the time of Schumann's mental breakdown until his death in 1856, Brahms and Clara tended to the ailing composer. The truth of the relationship between Brahms and Clara Schumann remains something of a mystery. Brahms never married. Clara Schumann never re-married following Robert's death. When Clara Schumann died in May of 1896, Brahms did not get to the funeral due to a missed train connection. He died the following April. Throughout his life, Brahms would sign letters "Frei aber froh" (Free but happy), until his last years when he signed "Frei aber einsam," (Free but lonely). One of the pall-bearers at Brahms' funeral was the composer Antonín Dvorák.

FRYDERYK CHOPIN (1810-1849).

Although composer and pianist Fryderyk Chopin was born to a French father and spent half of his life in Paris, he always defined himself by the land of his birth, Poland. Throughout his life he retained strong nationalistic feelings. Chopin the pianist achieved the status of an idol. His mystique was based in part on his cultured upbringing and in part on his fragile good looks. His sensitive nature, frail health, and self-imposed exile only intensified the public's fascination with him. In 1831, after receiving his training and achieving some success in Poland, Chopin moved to Paris. There he found himself one of many piano virtuosos. Although he quickly made a name for himself, his temperament and physical frailty, caused by tuberculosis that plagued him throughout much of his life, left him poorly suited to life as a performer. He gave only about 30 performances, many of which were private affairs. From 1838 to 1847 Chopin was romantically involved with novelist Georges Sand (Aurore Dudevant). The years of their stormy romance were his most productive as a composer. While Franz Lizst created works of grand proportions and brilliant virtuosity, Chopin remained a miniaturist, creating elegant, fluid melodies within the framework of small pieces. He was the only great composer who wrote almost exclusively for the piano. Chopin is set apart from other Romantic era composers by the fact that his works were not inspired by or based upon literature, works of art, or political ideals. Composition was difficult work for Chopin, who was a gifted improviser from his earliest days. He composed as he played, finding it painful to commit his work to paper. When Chopin and Georges Sand parted ways in 1847, the composer's frail health took a turn for the worse. He was further weakened by his 1848 concert tour of England. When he died in October of 1849, public fascination only increased, as evidenced by the nearly 3,000 mourners who attended his funeral.

CLAUDE DEBUSSY (1862-1918).

Claude Debussy saw rules as things to be tested. He repeatedly failed harmony exams during his student years, because of his refusal to accept that the rules were correct. Like many before him he took several tries to win the Priz de Rome. Debussy's musical language was affected by the music of Wagner (which he heard first-hand at the Bayreuth Festival) and Russian music. Another important event was exposure to the hazy harmonies of Javanese music. Yet the voice that he found was completely French. His music was as much a part of the Impressionist school of thought as the work of any painter. The composer also found his voice in periodic writings as a music critic. By breaking rules and composing in a style uniquely his own, Debussy led the way for a generation of French composers. His piano music was unlike anything the world had heard up until then, evoking a huge variety of sounds and harmonies from the keyboard. When Debussy died, after a long and painful battle with brain cancer, it seemed as though no one noticed. In fact, France was too consumed with war in 1918 to pause for the death of a composer, even the most important composer in the country.

ENRIQUE GRANADOS (1867-1916).

Spanish composer and pianist Enrique Granados once said that he was "not a musician but an artist." In fact, in addition to his musical abilities, Granados was also accomplished as a writer and a painter. After studies in Barcelona and Paris, Granados returned to Spain where he worked as a teacher, pianist and composer, writing a large number of pieces for voice and piano. His most successful composition was the 1911 piano suite entitled *Goyescas*, a set of virtuosic pieces inspired by paintings of Goya. Granados eventually expanded the music of the piano suite to create an opera, giving it the same title. The operatic version of *Goyescas* was performed at the Metropolitan Opera in New York in January of 1916. Granados was on hand for the successful premiere. President Woodrow Wilson requested that the composer present a recital at the White House. The performance made him alter his travel plans, missing a ship bound directly for Spain. Instead, following the concert he sailed for England, where he boarded the *Sussex* for Dieppe. In the middle of the English Channel the *Sussex* was torpedoed by a German submarine. Granados was picked up by a lifeboat, but when he saw his wife struggling in the water, he dove in to rescue her. Both of them drowned. In a letter to a friend, mailed from New York a few weeks before his death, Granados wrote, "I have a whole world of ideas. ...I am only now starting my work."

EDVARD GRIEG (1843-1907).

Edvard Grieg holds a unique position in music history as not just the most famous of Norwegian composers, but as one of the only Norwegian composers to have achieved an international reputation. Grieg drew upon traditional Norwegian folksongs for the inspiration and basis for many of his pieces. His incorporation of national folk music into classical forms inspired musicians throughout Europe to do the same with the traditional music of their own countries. Although Grieg's Piano Concerto in A Minor is his best known work, it is not typical of his style. Most of his pieces are small in scale, giving him a reputation as a miniaturist. Grieg's first music lessons came from his mother. When Norwegian violinist Ole Bull heard the teen-aged Grieg play the piano, he arranged for him to enter the Leipzig Conservatory in Germany. Although the young musician was terribly homesick, living so far from home, he enjoyed the opportunity to hear performances by such luminaries as Clara Schumann and Richard Wagner. After his studies in Germany, and later in Denmark, Grieg returned to Norway. Finding himself in demand throughout Europe, Grieg spent much of his career traveling. The recipient of honorary degrees from Cambridge and Oxford, Grieg was also honored as one of his country's foremost composers.

CHARLES TOMLINSON GRIFFES (1884-1920).

Born in Elmira, New York, Charles Tomlinson Griffes aspired to be a concert pianist. After beginning piano lessons under the tutelage of his sister, Griffes began studying with Mary Selena Broughton, who taught at the Elmira College. She encouraged his dream and financed his studies at the Stern Conservatory in Berlin. Although Griffes was quite successful at the piano, he found himself more interested in composition. He eventually withdrew from the conservatory, remaining in Berlin to study composition with composer Engelbert Humperdinck. Griffes moved back to the United States in 1907, and to earn a living he became director of music at the Hackley School in Tarrytown, New York. Although Griffes' early music is strongly tied to the German romantic tradition, his later works lean more toward the subtlety of the impressionists, with even later works turning toward free use of dissonance. He was constantly experimenting and searching for a style that suited his personality and temperament. Griffes composed a large number of pieces for voice and piano, as well as works for piano, chamber music, orchestral pieces and works for the stage. The composer died at age 35, from what was originally reported as tuberculosis. It was later explained that his death was caused by abscesses of the lungs, which had stemmed from influenza.

SCOTT JOPLIN (1868-1917).

Joplin's father was freed from slavery only five years before his famous son. Although composer and pianist Scott Joplin would come to be know as the "King of Ragtime," it would be more than a half century after his death before his genius would be recognized. Joplin was one of the principal innovators in ragtime, a highly syncopated music that began as a dance accompaniment at clubs in the St. Louis area. Ragtime came to popularity in the Midwest at about the same time jazz began in New Orleans. Joplin landed a job as a saloon pianist in St. Louis in 1885. Following his appearance at the Columbian Exposition in 1893, he settled in Sedalia, Missouri, and began composing. Although his "Maple Leaf Rag" was initially turned down by publishers because of its difficulty, it proved to be the piece that brought Joplin his first taste of musical notability. By 1908 Joplin was in New York City, turning his attention to composing larger works. He tried his hand at an opera, *A Guest of Honor*. His dream of writing opera consumed him, taking up much time and money. No one was particularly interested in producing an opera by an African-American at that time. He finally used his own funds to produce his opera *Treemonisha* at an inadequate hall in Harlem in 1915. The performance was a failure. Following the *Treemonisha* premiere, Joplin's mental health deteriorated steadily until he was committed to the Manhattan State Hospital. He died there, in poverty, in 1917. His music was largely forgotten by the 1970s when his complete works were published by the New York Public Library. A number of respected concert pianists began to program his works. The film *The Sting* employed much of his music, and spearheaded a popular Joplin revival. *Treemonisha* was resurrected in 1972, and eventually played on Broadway. Joplin, finally recognized as an innovator in American music, was awarded a posthumous Pulitzer Prize in 1976.

FRANZ LISZT (1811-1886).

Critics of the Hungarian composer/pianist Franz Liszt, the most famous pianist in history, accused him of composing music that was little more than a vehicle for self-promotion. He was the greatest pianist of his age, and judging from accounts of his playing and the music he composed for himself, he may have been the greatest pianist who has ever lived. His limitless piano technique set a standard for concert pianists that remains in effect to this day. Liszt was a larger-than-life character who generously supported the work of other composers and single-handedly invented the modern piano recital. His romantic life was legendary. He lived for many years with the Countess Marie D'Agoult, although she was married to another man. Liszt fathered two children with the Countess (one of whom would later marry conductor Hans von Bülow, only to leave him for composer Richard Wagner). Liszt later entered a romance with Princess Carolyne Sayn-Wittgenstein, for whom he left the concert stage and became Kapellmeister to the Grand Duke of Weimar. For a decade he lived in Weimar, writing and refining much of the music for which he is known. In his later years he took minor orders in the Roman Catholic church. Liszt was a generous teacher and taught a large number of students, exerting a profound influence over music-making in Europe for decades. He was also a conductor, and lead premieres of new works by Wagner, Berlioz and Verdi. As a composer Liszt looked to the future. His melodrama, "Der träurige Mönch," an atonal composition based on a tone row, clearly foreshadowed the subsequent work (decades later) of Arnold Schönberg. Public fascination with Liszt, the most famous celebrity in Europe, continued throughout his life. Not long before he died he celebrated his seventy-fifth birthday by embarking on a Julilee tour that received press coverage around the world.

FELIX MENDELSSOHN (1809-1847).

While most of Mendelssohn's colleagues could tell stories of their battles with family over choice of career and even more tales of their financial struggles as musicians, Felix Mendelssohn could only listen. He was born into a wealthy family that supported his goals in music from the very first. Even in their conversion from Judaism to Christianity, which the family had long considered, they were spurred to action by thoughts of their son's future. It was at the time of their conversion that they changed the family surname to Mendelssohn-Bartholdy. Mendelssohn set out on his musical career with two clear goals. He wanted to re-introduce the largely forgotten music of old masters such as Bach to the public, and he dreamed of opening a first-rate conservatory. At the age of twenty he conducted a pioneering performance of Bach's *St. Matthew Passion*, the first of many such concerts he would lead. A few years later he founded and directed the Leipzig Conservatory. As a composer, Mendelssohn combined the expressive ideals of the Romantics with the traditional forms of the Classical era. He is remembered both as one of the great Romantic composers and one of the last of classicists. In his career Mendelssohn found success at an early age, and remained highly successful until his death. His sister Fanny, to whom he was exceptionally close, died suddenly on May 14, 1847. Shortly after he got the news of his sister's death, Mendelssohn fell unconscious, having burst a blood vessel in his head. Although he recovered from this incident, he was terribly diminished by the illness. His health and mental state deteriorated until his death on November 4 that same year. Memorial services for the great conductor/composer were held in most German cities, as well as in various cities in Great Britain, where he had become quite a celebrity.

WOLFGANG AMADEUS MOZART (1756-1791).

It is exceptional for nature to produce such a prodigy as Mozart. Playing capably at age three, composing at five and concertizing throughout Europe at age six, Mozart was clearly remarkable, even for a prodigy. But for nature to have placed two prodigies in one household is beyond belief. Mozart's sister Marianne (Nannerl), a few years older than Mozart, was also a prodigy and was also featured on these concert tours. The young musician's parents moved heaven and earth to further offer Mozart every opportunity to perform and study abroad. They traveled Europe incessantly. As an adult, Mozart had difficulties in his relationships with his employers, and with colleagues. Pop culture has presented us with a caricature image of the composer, thanks in great part to the film *Amadeus*, in which he is painted as a freakish, spoiled child who refused to grow up. He was, in fact, impetuous and, likely as a result of his star status as a child, often difficult to deal with. But there was more depth of personality and musicianship than the film attempted to convey. Mozart was known to complete an entire symphony in a single carriage ride, yet he chafed at accusations that it was not work for him to compose. Another factor in the exaggerated stories of his character was his inability to handle financial matters. Although he was well paid for many of his compositions, he was in constant financial difficulty. He was frequently forced to borrow money from family and friends. Mozart, who more than any other composer represents the Classical era, tried his hand at virtually every musical genre available, and succeeded across the board. In 1791 Mozart received a commission to compose a requiem. According to the terms, the source of the commission was to remain anonymous. The piece proved to be the composer's own requiem, in that he died of a 'fever" before it was completed. The circumstance of his death, and the anonymous commission, gave rise to great speculation at the time, and a film some two centuries later. In the mid twentieth century, the composer Richard Strauss is said to have laid a hand on a copy of Mozart's Clarinet Quintet and said, "I would give anything to have written this."

IGNACY JAN PADEREWSKI (1860-1941).

Known to audiences as a piano virtuoso and a composer, Ignacy Jan Paderewski was also known to Polish citizens as a tireless fighter for Polish political interests. He served as the Prime Minister of Poland for several years. In the early years of the twentieth century, Paderewski was making successful concert tours of Europe, North and South America, Australia, New Zealand and South Africa, while devoting his summers to composition. Much of the money he made from these extensive tours went back to charities in Poland. He became politically active on behalf of Poland in about 1910, leaving the concert stage in 1918 to devote himself to politics. He was made Prime Minister of Poland in 1919 and, as representative of Poland, was one of the signers of the Treaty of Versailles. In 1922 he returned to the concert stage, using his summers to teach. When the Nazis invaded Poland, in the early years of World War II, Paderewski used his celebrity and political status to take up his country's cause abroad. He campaigned heavily in the United States for assistance for Poland. It was during this endeavor that he died, in New York. He was given a state burial at Arlington National Cemetery. During his lifetime, Paderewski's name was synonymous with sparkling, virtuosic playing. Among the many honors awarded him by various governments was the highest military honor of the Polish government, the Cross of the Virtuti Militari. It was awarded posthumously. Although Paderewski's compositions include an opera and several chamber, orchestral and vocal works, the vast majority of his pieces were written for piano. Throughout his career he was very supportive of young Polish composers. He was particularly famous for exquisitely crafted miniatures for piano.

SERGEI RACHMANINOFF (1873-1943).

Once described by composer Igor Stravinsky as "a six-and-a-half-foot-tall scowl," Sergei Rachmaninoff's stern visage was a trademark of sorts. Rachmaninoff first found fame as a pianist, touring throughout his native Russia to critical acclaim. His compositions won notice in those early years as well, including a Moscow Conservatory Gold Medal in composition. Yet the 1897 premiere of his Symphony No. 1 was a complete failure, due in large part to poor conducting by Alexander Glazunov. The dismal reception of the piece sent Rachmaninoff into a three-year creative slump that he overcame through hypnosis. During those three years he began conducting, earning international respect for his work on the podium. When his Symphony No. 1 received its London premiere in 1909, it was a huge success. Rachmaninoff made his first U.S. tour in 1909. On the tour he featured his Piano Concerto No. 3, which he had written expressly for his American audiences. Rachmaninoff fled Russia in the wake of the October Revolution of 1917. He brought his family to America where he continued to concertize, but did not compose for nearly a decade. After years of touring, Rachmaninoff decided that the 1942-43 concert season would have to be his last. In January of 1943 he began to suffer from an illness diagnosed as pleurisy. He gave what was to be his final performance on February 17. He then returned to his Beverly Hills home where he died of cancer on March 28.

MAURICE RAVEL (1875-1937).

Along with composer Claude Debussy, Maurice Ravel was at the heart of a re-birth of a French school of classical music. Ravel's career got off to a rocky start. In addition to five failed attempts at winning the Prix de Rome, and some scandal involved in the judging of at least one of his attempts, he found himself in the midst of an even greater scandal as a young professional. He was accused of plagiarizing the music of Debussy. While he had not in fact plagiarized, the storm raged throughout Paris as musicians took sides in the debate. In the end it all blew over. The result was that much of France's music-loving population had listened closely to works by the young composer and had liked what they had heard. Ravel was suddenly famous. While his contemporary Debussy ventured ever farther from traditional tonality and formal structure, Ravel remained more of a traditionalist. He combined the traditional and the contemporary, infusing his music with flavors of Spanish and Asian culture. He included tastes of the gypsy music of Europe and the new sounds of jazz that were coming out of America. He was also a skilled orchestrator, creating the well-known orchestration of Musorgsky's *Pictures at an Exhibition*. Ravel was eventually stricken with a degenerative brain disease that left him unable to sign his own name. In desperation he underwent a risky brain surgery, from which he never awoke.

ANTON RUBINSTEIN (1829-1894).

Remembered as one of the greatest pianists of the nineteenth century, Anton Rubinstein was a child prodigy. His younger brother Nikolay was a pianistic prodigy as well. Anton gave his first public performance at the age of ten, beginning a concert tour of Europe the following year. He began his adult professional career in 1854 with a wildly successful tour of Europe. As a pianist Rubinstein was often compared favorably to Franz Liszt. By 1872 he was touring the United States with Wieniawski, and was the most sought-after pianist in the world. But Rubinstein also saw himself as a composer, writing enormous amounts of music: operas, concertos, chamber works, choral and vocal music as well as numerous pieces for piano. He would scribble down music in haste, relying on his famous name to sell the pieces rather than taking the time to refine and polish them. Of the mountain of pieces he wrote, only two, the "Melody in F" and the 1871 opera *Demon* achieved anything more than fleeting success. Rubinstein was also a controversial figure in Russian musical circles. Feeling that the nationalism that was appearing in Russian music was amateurish at best, he established the St. Petersburg Conservatory. Through his efforts as an educator, he was pivotal in raising musical standards throughout Russia. One of his many students was Tchaikovsky.

DOMENICO SCARLATTI (1685-1757).

Domenico Scarlatti, christened Giuseppe Domenico, went by his second name throughout his life. He is not to be confused with his nephew Giuseppe, also a composer, who was born more than three decades later. The sixth of composer Alessandro Scarlatti's ten children, Domenico spent many years chafing under the heavy hand of his domineering father. His first professional position was that of organist and composer of the vice-regal court at Naples, where his father was the *maestro di cappelli*. Later he worked as his father's assistant in Rome. Eventually the younger Scarlatti won independence, but only through the extreme measure of a legal decree. Little is known about Domenico's personal life other than that he married twice, had nine children and formed a strong association with Handel. In 1719 he took a position in Portugal. He moved to Madrid in 1733, where he remained for the rest of his life, often using the altered Spanish version of his name, Domingo Escarlatti. Over the course of his life Scarlatti composed more than 550 keyboard sonatas, 17 sinfonias, 12 operas, three masses, and some 70 cantatas in addition to other sacred works.

FRANZ SCHUBERT (1797-1828).

The story of Schubert's life reads like a heartbreaking novel. Now hailed as one of the great Romantic composers, not one of Schubert's symphonies was performed during his lifetime. It was five decades after his death before any of them were published. Schubert, the son of a school headmaster, was not a virtuoso musician. Although his musical abilities were readily apparent to his teachers, his inability to perform left him with little means to support himself. He taught in his father's school for a time, but was miserable in that job. Schubert studied with Salieri, who was astounded by the young composer's abilities. After writing his first symphony at age fifteen, Schubert presented Salieri with a completed, fully orchestrated opera two years later. Schubert lived less than thirty-two years, yet he composed a phenomenal amount of music, including some six hundred songs. One hundred and forty-four of those songs date from the year 1815, a year in which he was teaching at his father's school. After Schubert left his father's school, he had the good fortune to collect a small group of devoted friends and supporters. The friends would periodically organize evenings of the composer's music, which came to be known as "Schubertiades." Schubert's health began to fail as early as 1822. When he died, at age thirty-one, he was viewed as a composer of songs. It was not the enormous number of songs that earned him this mistaken designation so much as the fact that almost none of his other music had been performed during his lifetime. In addition to the songs, Schubert completed seven symphonies and left one unfinished. He wrote a number of operas, although these are far from his best works. He also wrote choral works, chamber music and piano pieces. In accordance with his dying wish, he was buried beside Beethoven, whom he had idolized and at whose funeral he had served as a torch-bearer.

ROBERT SCHUMANN (1810-1856).

Robert Schumann's dream was to become a pianist. As the son of a German bookseller and writer, he grew up surrounded by literature and instilled with a love of music. His world crumbled however, when he was just sixteen, with the death of his father and the subsequent suicide of his sister. Schumann entered law school, but spent most of his time studying music. In 1830 he moved into the household of his piano teacher, Friedrich Wieck. Soon afterwards, his left hand began to trouble him. His career dreams were shattered when his left hand became permanently crippled. He turned his energies to composition, making a name as a music critic as well. An inspired critic, he founded the music journal *Neue Zeitschrift für Musik*, in 1834; he often wrote under the pseudonyms "Florestan" and "Eusebius." Schumann fell in love with his teacher's daughter, Clara Wieck, a highly acclaimed concert pianist. Clara's father fought vigorously against the romance. Schumann married Clara in 1840, but only after he had taken his case to the courts. In the year he was married, the composer wrote some 150 songs, turning to orchestral music the following year. Schumann suffered from bouts of terrible depression, which became progressively worse with time. In 1854 he attempted suicide. Unable to function any longer, he was then placed in an asylum, where he spent the last two years of his life. His wife, along with his friend, the young composer Johannes Brahms, looked after him in those final years.

ALEXANDER SKRYABIN (1872-1915).

Pianist and composer Alexander Skryabin, a classmate of Rachmaninoff, is remembered for the unflinching modernism of his later works and for his mystical theories relating color to musical pitches. He was born into an aristocratic Russian family and was raised by an aunt, grandmother and great-aunt following the death of his mother. The women in Skryabin's life doted on him, catering to his every need and whim while fostering his ego-maniacal, fastidious tendencies. In later years he depended on his managers for such cater-ing. Skryabin was a short man, whose small hands were unable to reach more than an octave on the piano—a surprising fact, considering the reach required in some of his music. At the time of his death, which was caused by an infected boil on his lip, Skryabin had ambitious plans for a quasi-religious work entitled *Mysterium*. The work was intended to unite all of the various arts. Much of the music dating from the last four years of the composer's life was written in preparation for this piece, using the floating dissonance of the "mystic" chord (C-F#-Bb-E-A-D). Much of Skryabin's earlier work was heavily influ-enced by the music of Chopin. As his own style developed he began to write more ornate and dissonant music, often making use of whole-tone passages and harmonies.

PYOTR IL'YICH TCHAIKOVSKY (1840-1893).

It is a curious twist of fate that the composer of so bombastic a work as the *1812 Overture* should have been an extremely fragile individual. Exceptionally sensitive from childhood, Tchaikovsky eventually deteriorated into a precarious emotional state. Tchaikovsky's musical abilities were already quite evident by age five, as was his hypersensitivity. His mother died when he was fourteen, a painful event that some say prompted him to com-pose. Over the years he was plagued by sexual scandals and episodes we might call "ner-vous breakdowns" today. Historians have uncovered evidence that his death, which was officially listed as having been caused by cholera, was actually a suicide. Many believe that the composer knowingly drank water tainted with cholera. Tchaikovsky's work stands as some of the most essentially Russian music in the classical repertoire, yet he was not a part of the Russian nationalistic school. In fact he was treated quite cruelly by critics of his day. "Tchaikovsky's Piano Concerto No. 1, like the first pancake, is a flop," wrote a St. Petersburg critic in 1875. A Boston critic claimed that his Symphony No. 6 ("Pathétique") "...threads all the foul ditches and sewers of human despair; it is as unclean as music can well be." For all the vehement criticism the composer received during his lifetime, his works are now among the best loved of the classical repertoire. His ballet *The Nutcracker* is an international holiday classic, while *Swan Lake* is a staple in the repertoire of ballet companies throughout the world. His *1812 Overture* is among the most recognizable of all classical pieces. In 1893 the composer completed work on his Symphony No. 6. The first movement dealt with themes of passion, the second with romance, the third with disillu-sionment and the finale with death. The piece was premiered on October 28. Nine days later the composer was dead.

Prelude and Fugue in B-flat Major
from THE WELL-TEMPERED CLAVIER, BOOK I

Johann Sebastian Bach
1685–1750
BWV 866

PRELUDE

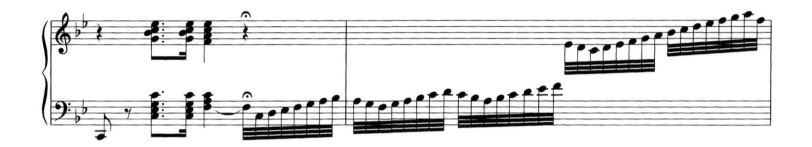

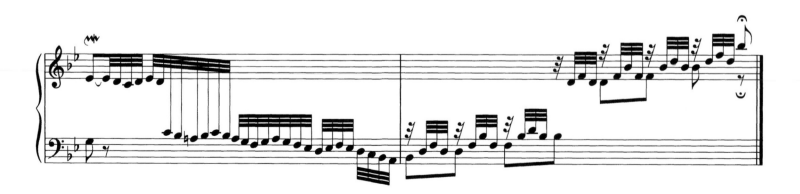

FUGUE (3 Voices)

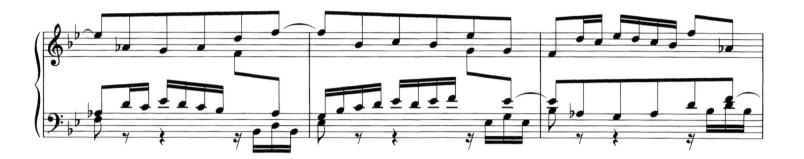

Rondo a capriccio in G Major
("Rage Over a Lost Penny")

Ludwig van Beethoven
1770–1827
Op. 129

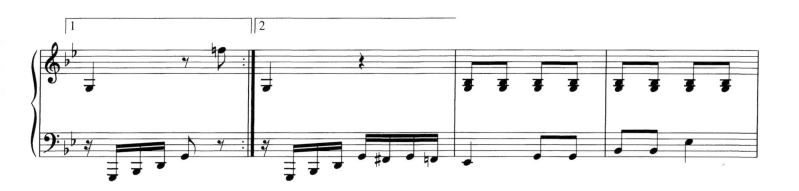

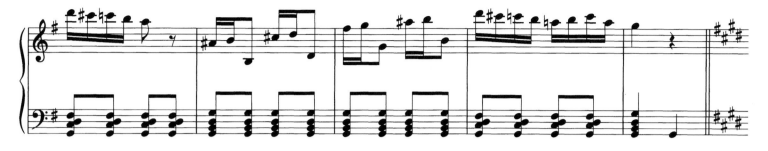

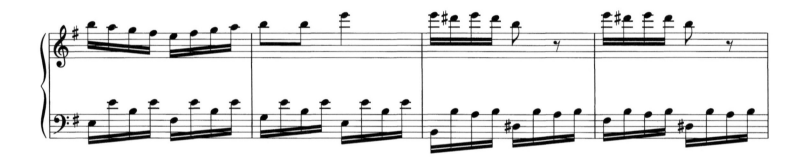

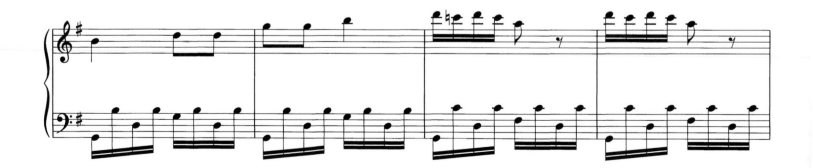

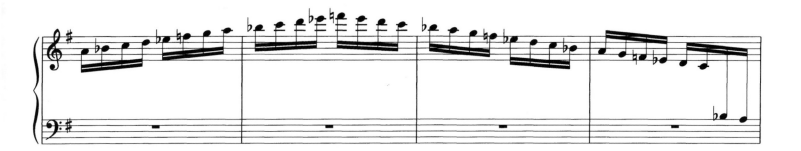

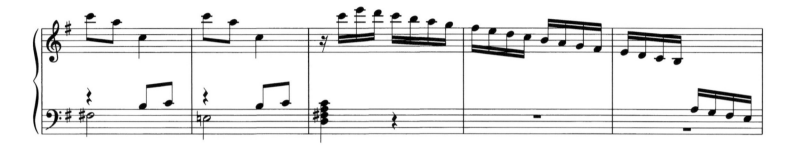

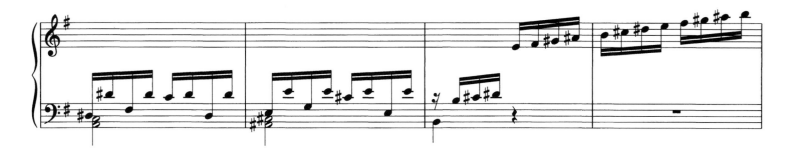

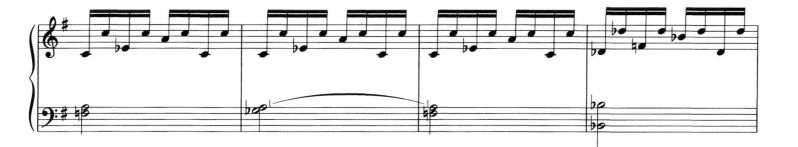

Romanian Folk Dances

Béla Bartók
1881–1945
Sz. 56

1. Dance with Sticks

Allegro moderato, ♩ = 100*

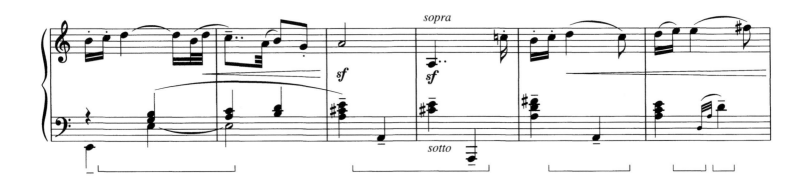

* The metronome markings are Bartók's.

2. Peasant Costume

Allegro, ♩ = 144

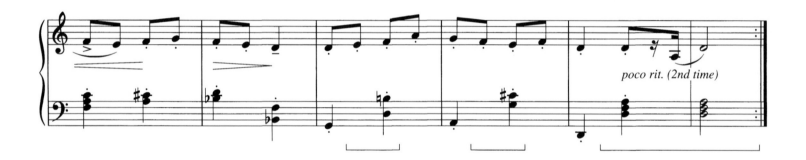

poco rit. (2nd time)

3. Stamping Dance

Andante, ♩ = 108

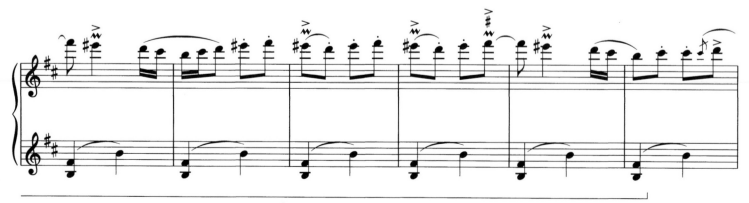

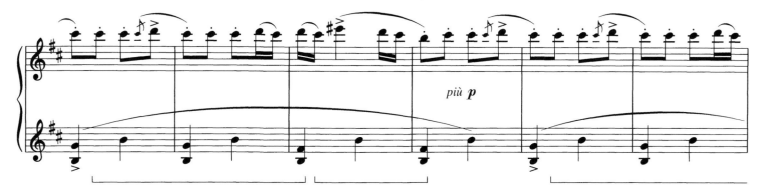

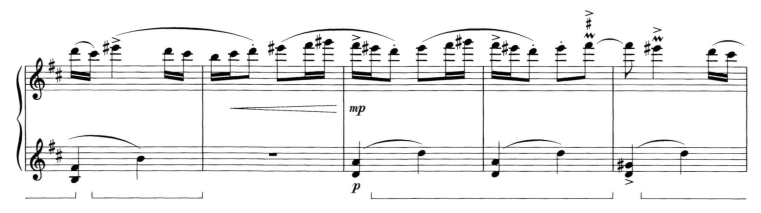

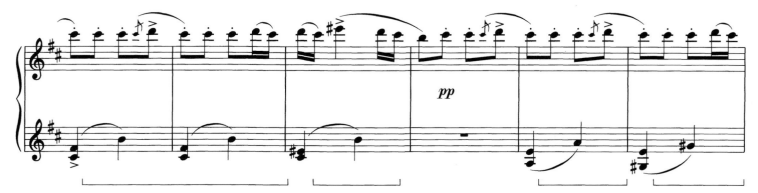

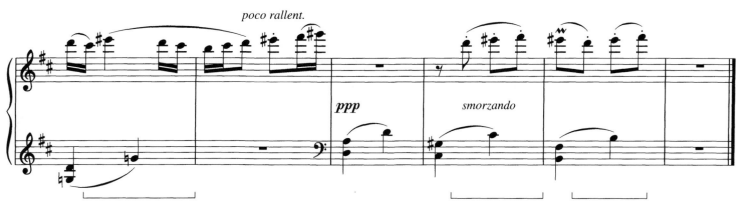

4. Song of the Mountain Horn

Moderato, ♩ = 100

5. Romanian Polka

Allegro, ♩ = 146

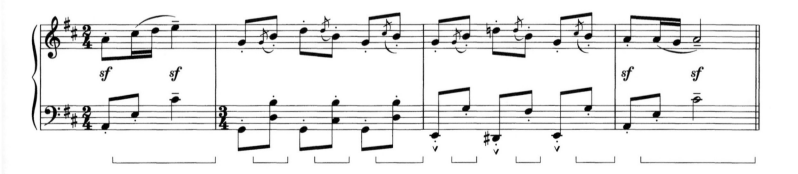

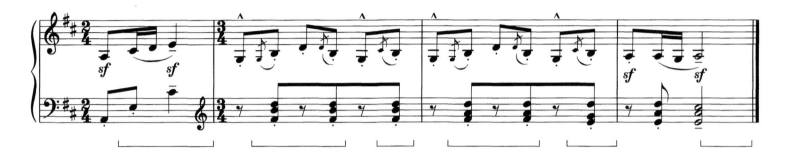

6. Fast Dance

Allegro, ♩ = 146

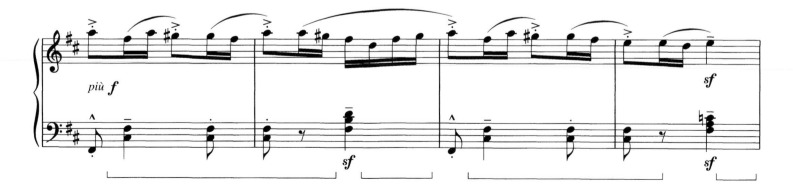

46

Più allegro, ♩ = 152

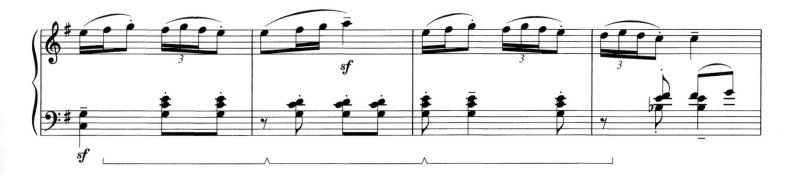

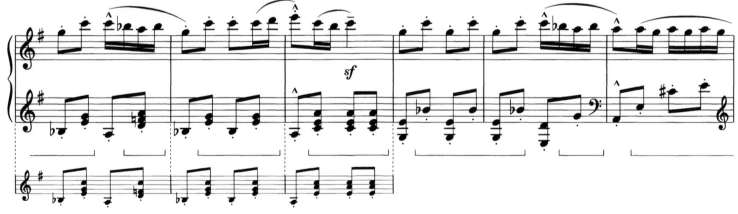

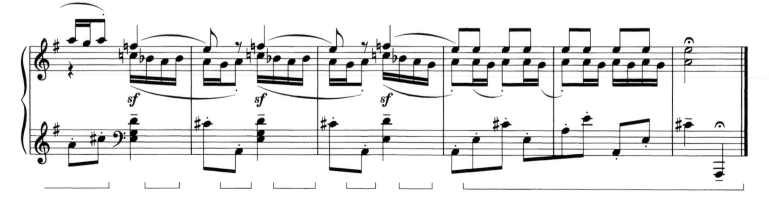

Rhapsody in G Minor

Johannes Brahms
1833–1897
Op. 79, No. 2

Molto passionato, ma non troppo Allegro

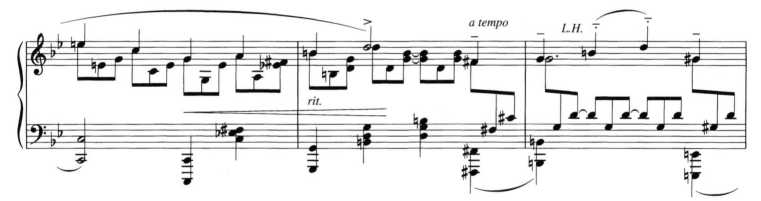

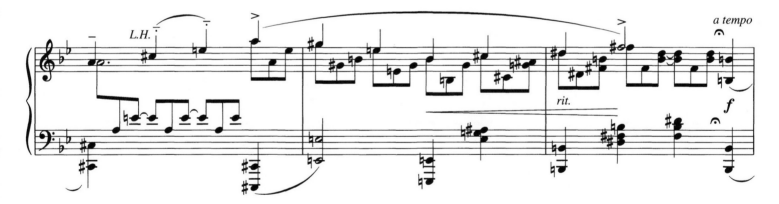

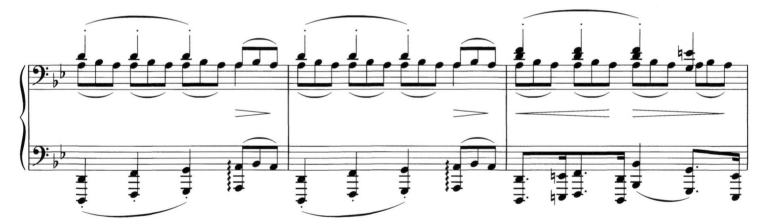

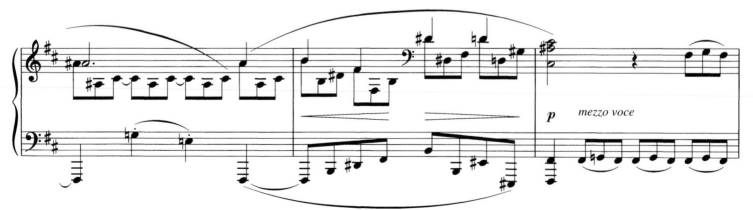

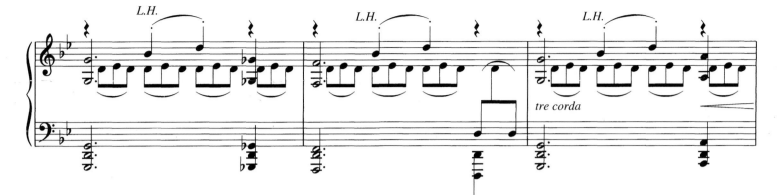

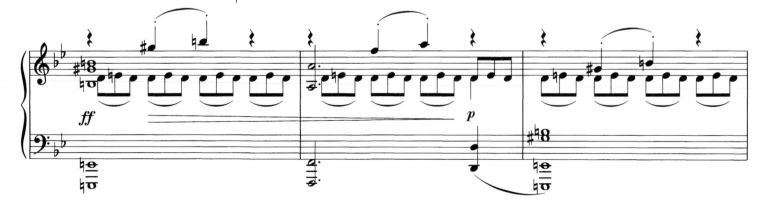

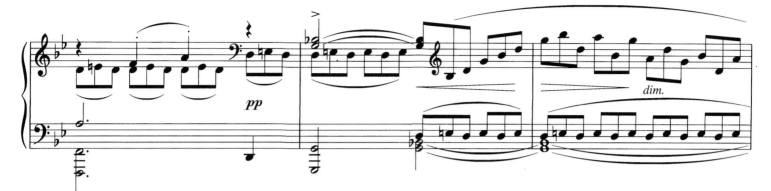

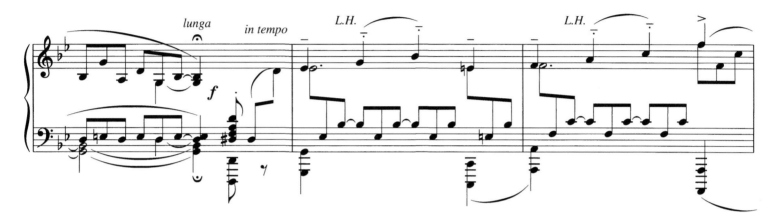

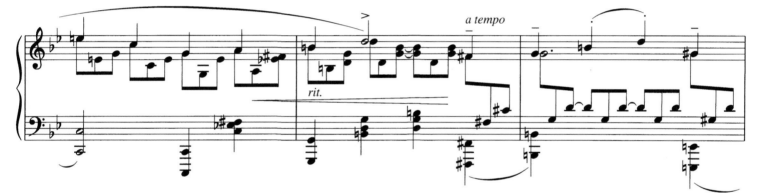

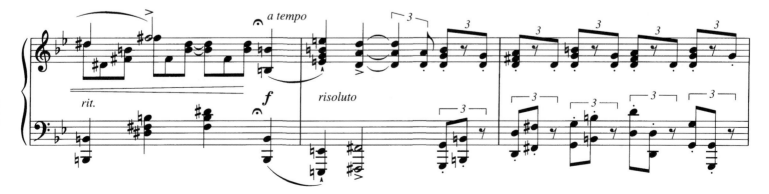

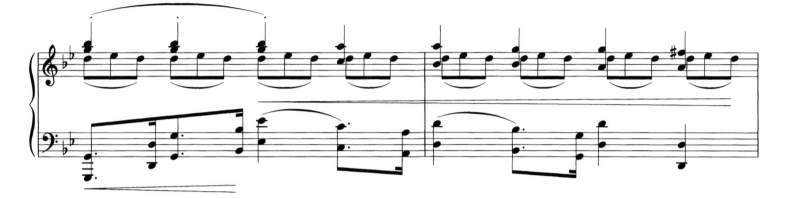

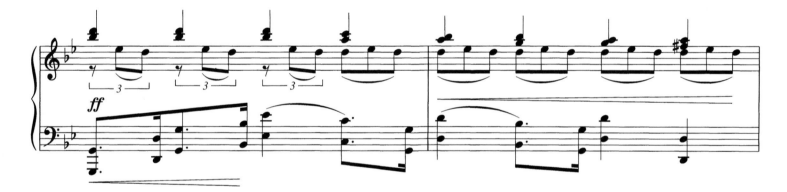

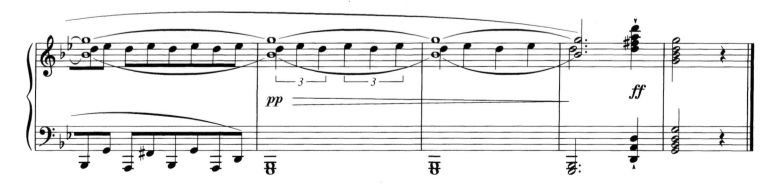

Intermezzo in A Major

Johannes Brahms
1833–1897
Op. 118, No. 2

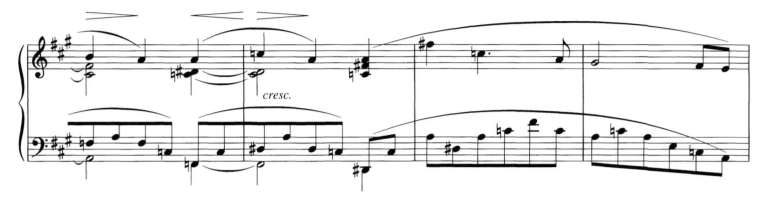

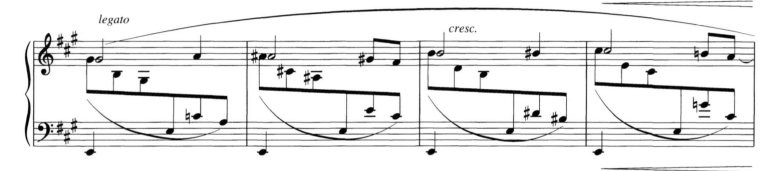

cresc., un poco animato

più lento

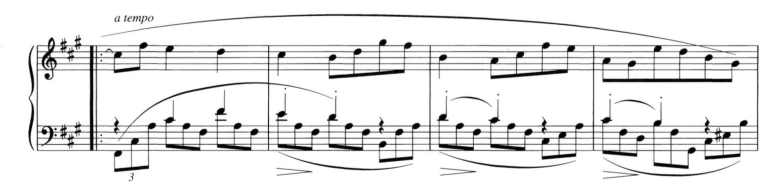

a tempo

rit.

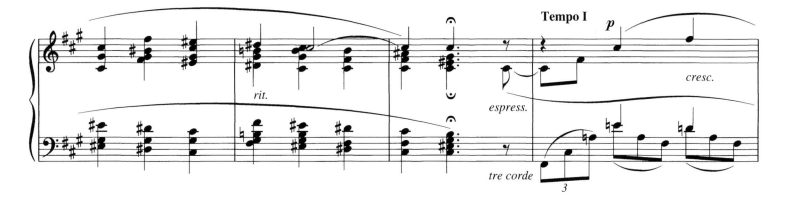

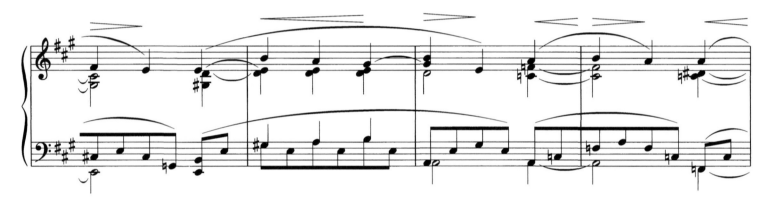

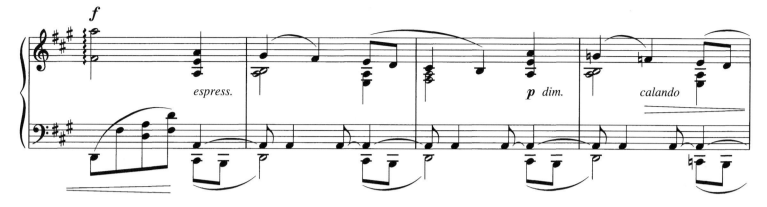

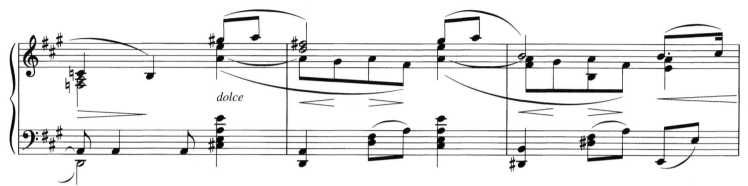

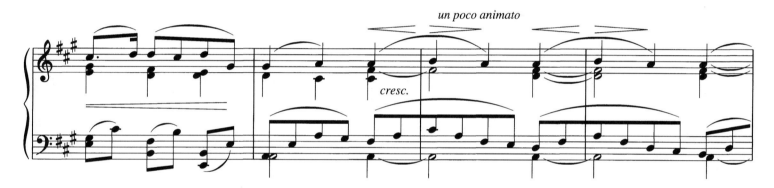

Intermezzo in A Minor

Johannes Brahms
1833–1897
Op. 118, No. 1

Allegro non assai, ma molto appassionato

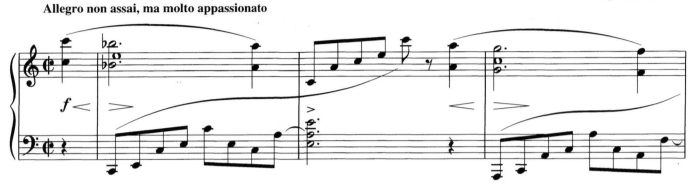

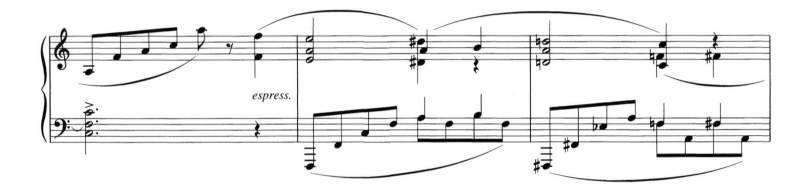

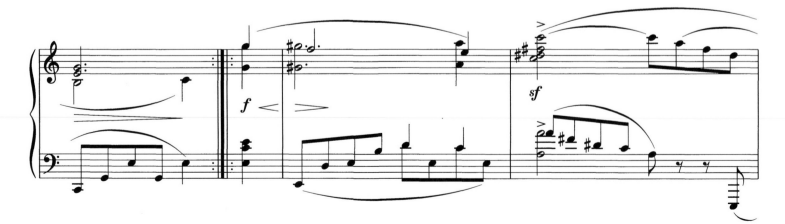

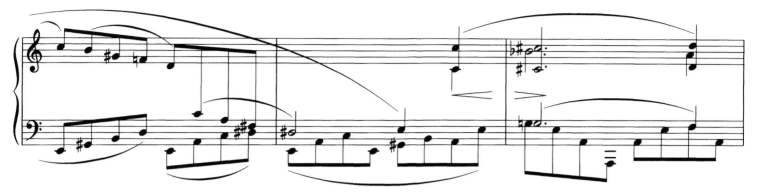

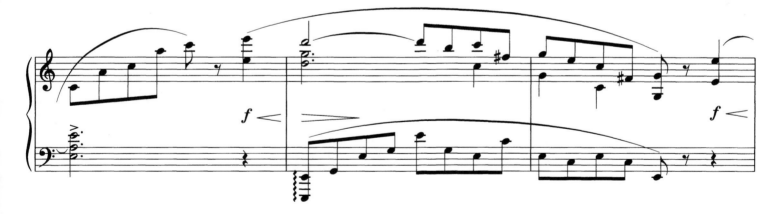

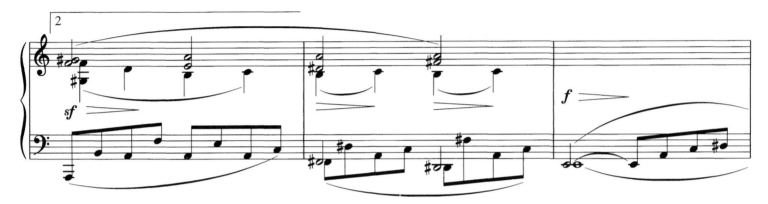

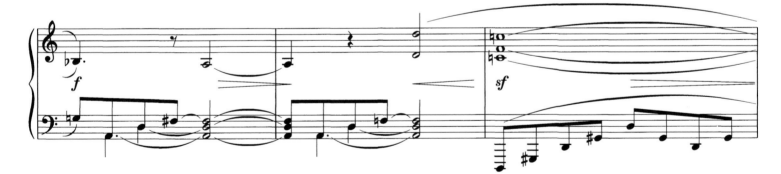

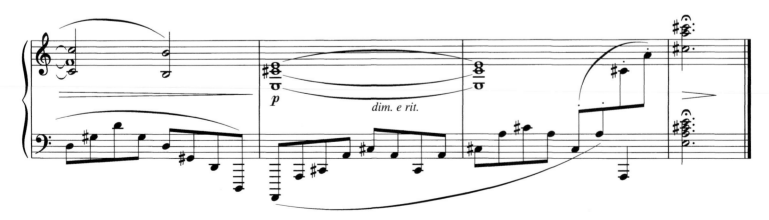

Intermezzo in E Major

Johannes Brahms
1833–1897
Op. 116, No. 6

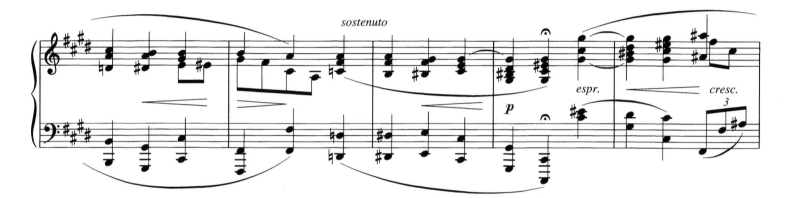

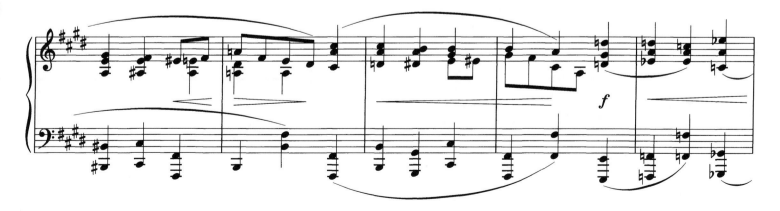

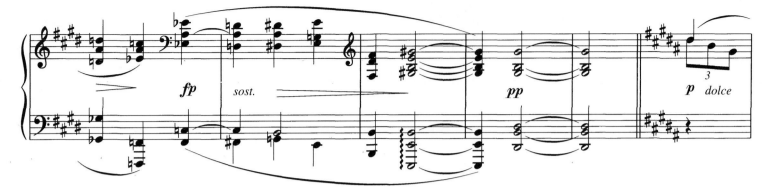

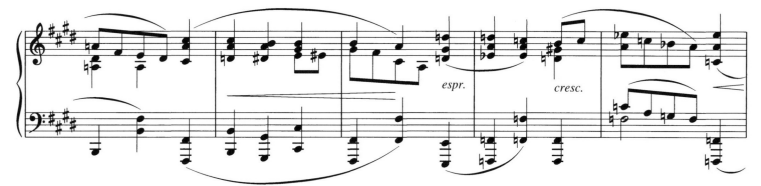

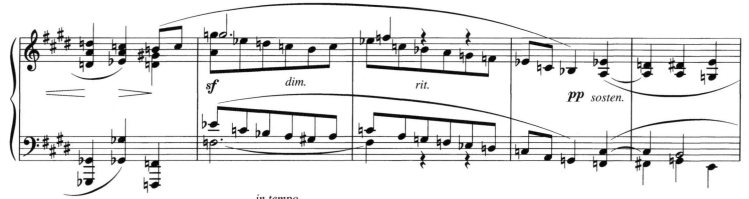

Mazurka in A Minor

Fryderyk Chopin
1810–1849
Op. 17, No. 4

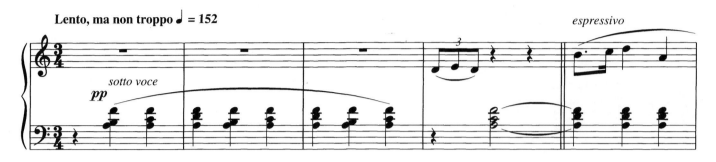

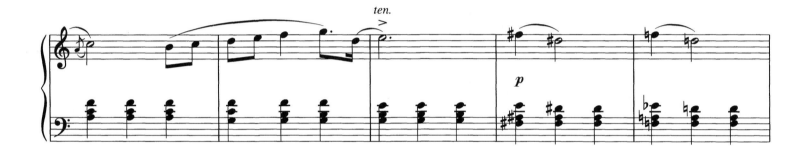

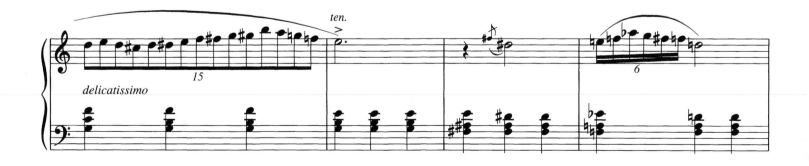

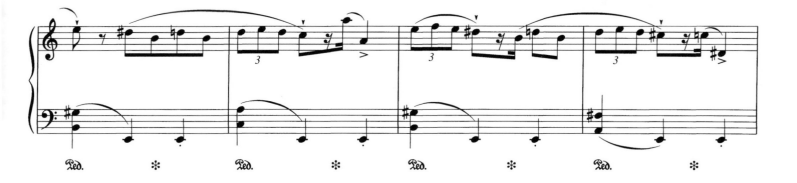

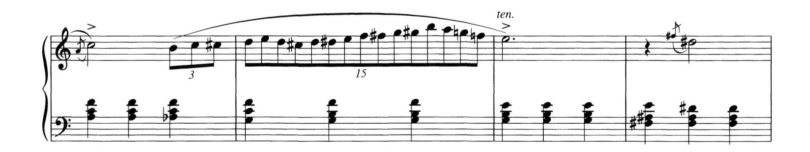

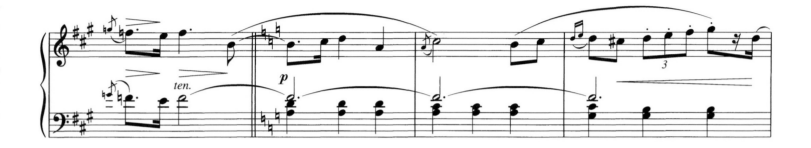

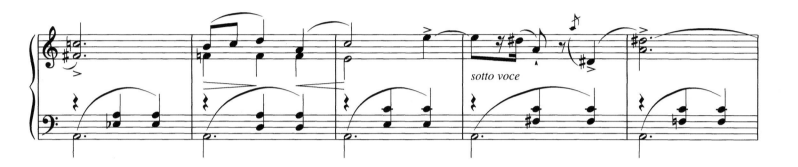

sotto voce

sempre più piano

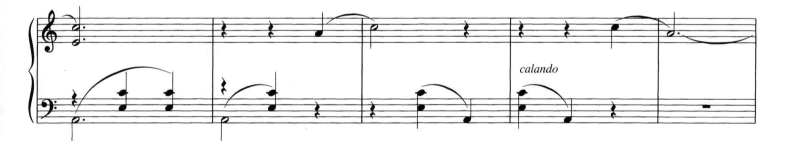

calando

perdendosi

Nocturne in C Minor

Fryderyk Chopin
1810–1849
Op. 48, No. 1

Poco più lento

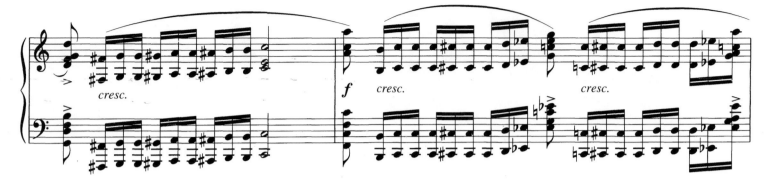

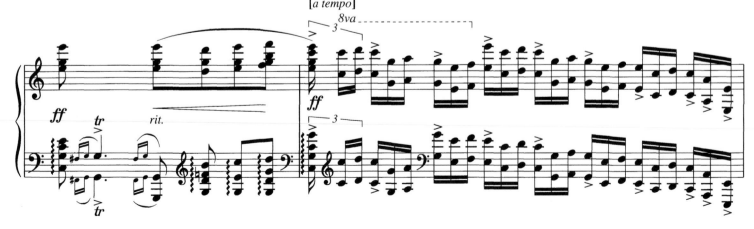

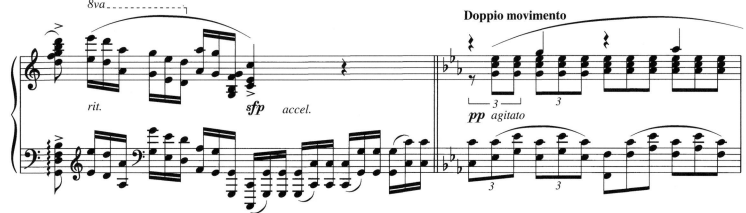

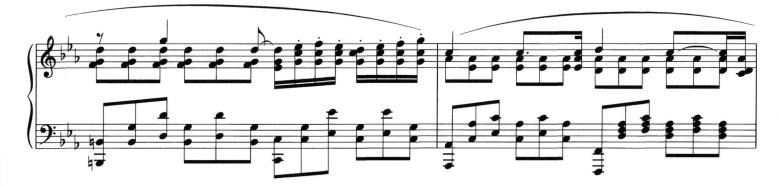

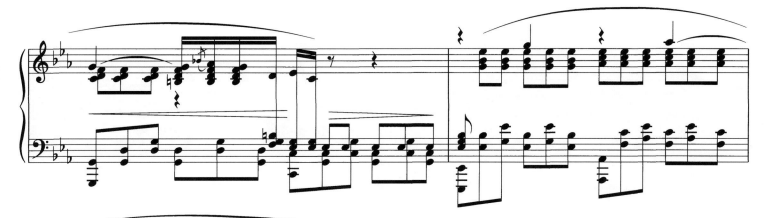

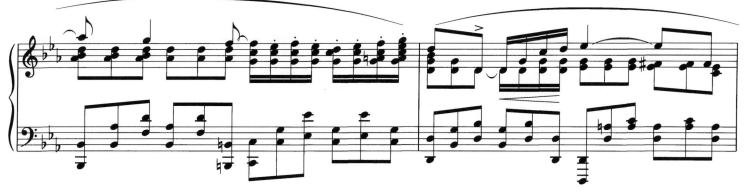

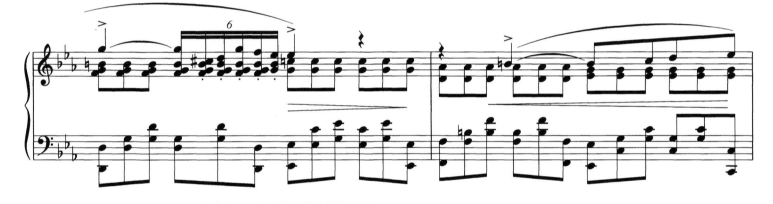

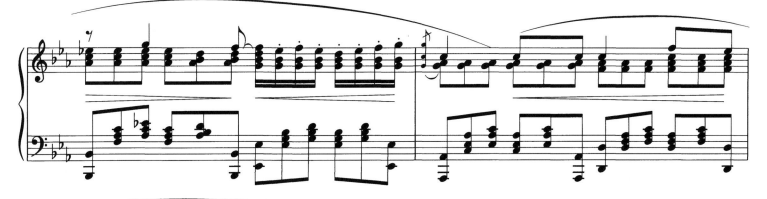

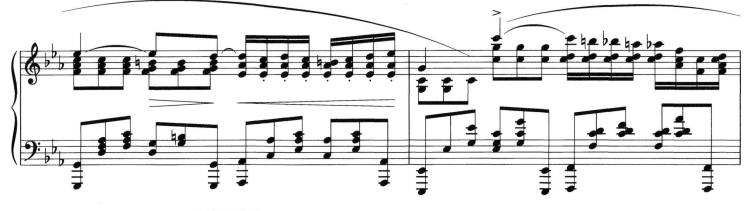

Polonaise Militaire

Fryderyk Chopin
1810–1849
Op. 40, No. 1

Allegro con brio

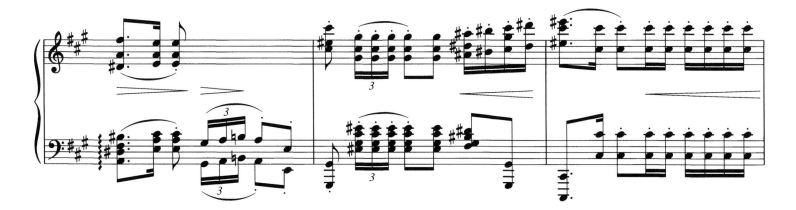

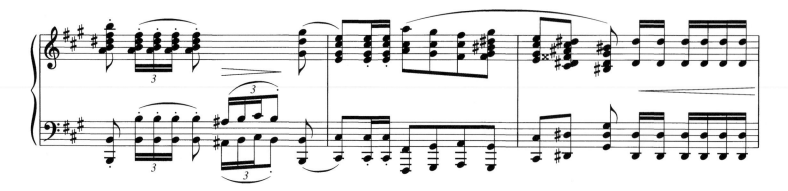

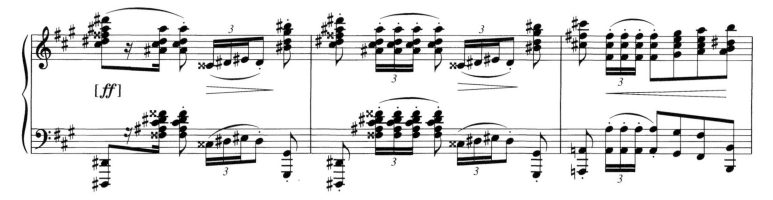

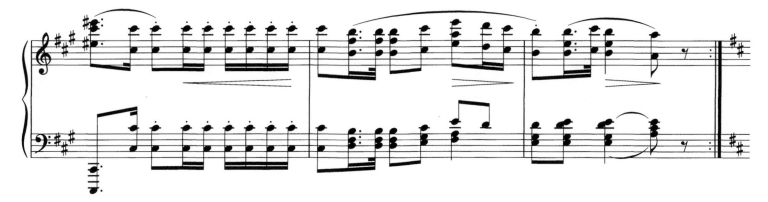

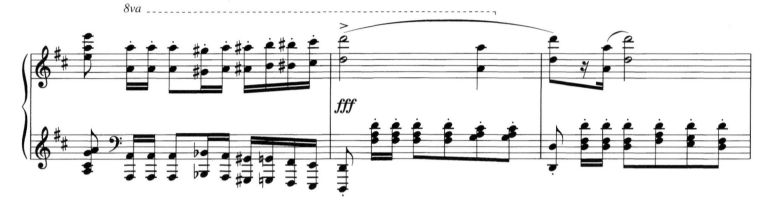

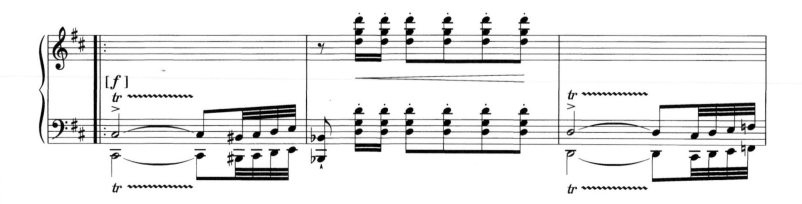

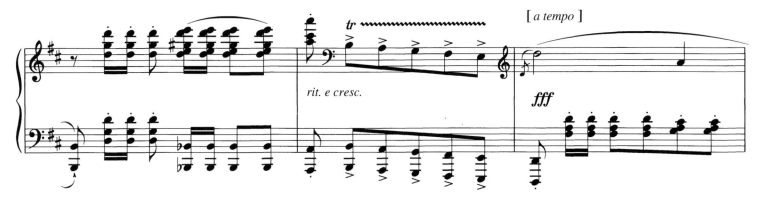

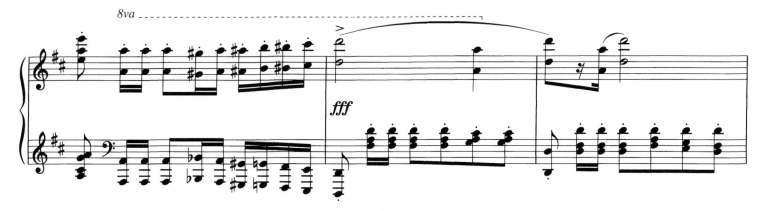

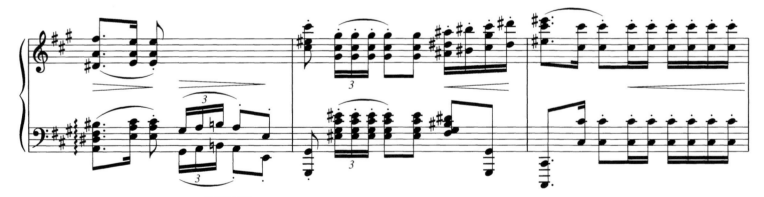

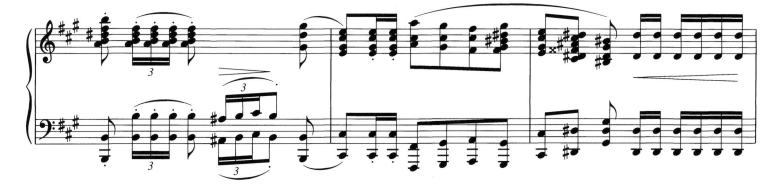

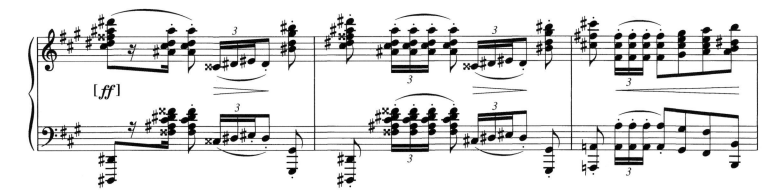

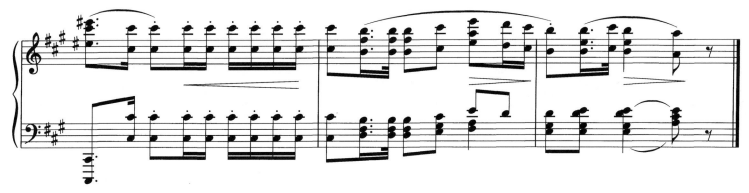

Waltz in C-sharp Minor

Fryderyk Chopin
1810–1849
Op. 64, No. 2

Tempo giusto

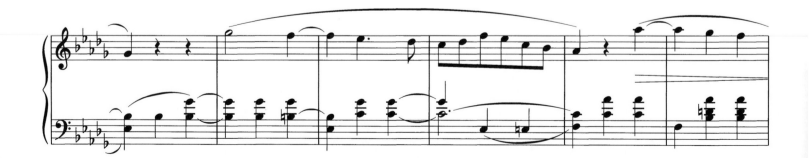

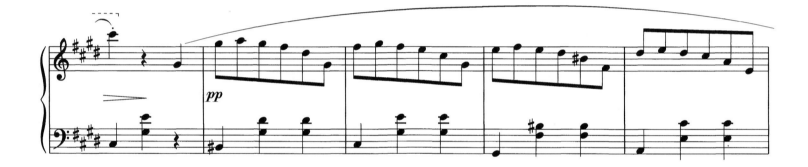

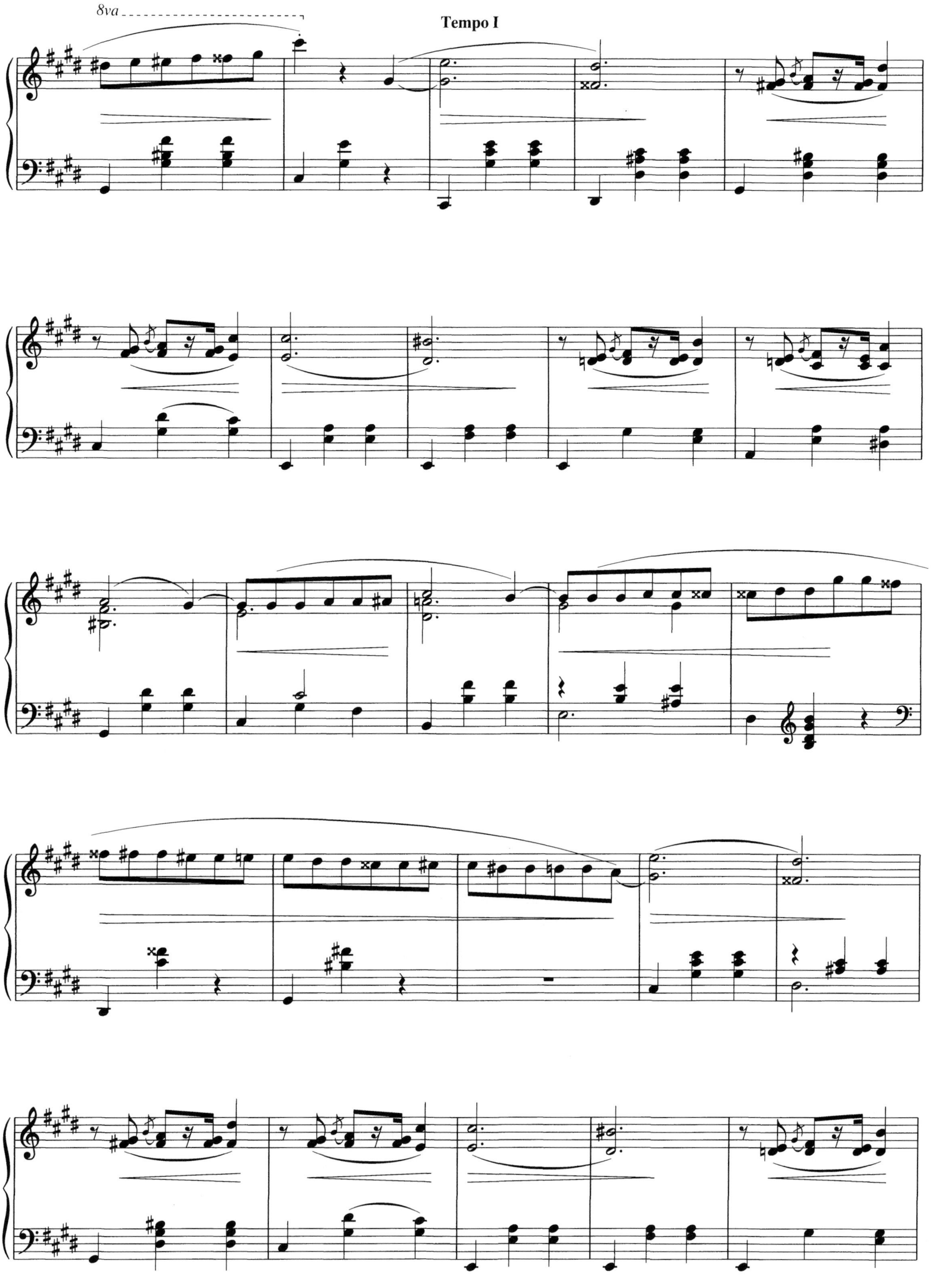
8va
Tempo I

Più mosso

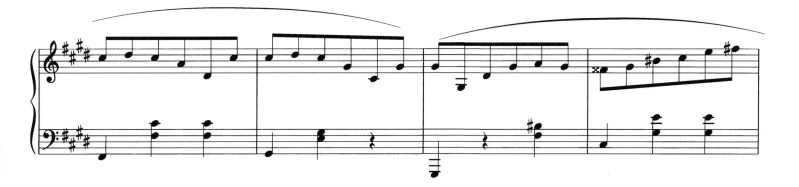

Minstrels

Claude Debussy
1862–1918

Modéré *(nerveux et avec humour)*

Cédez **au Mouvement**

Cédez **au Mouvement** *(un peu plus allant)*

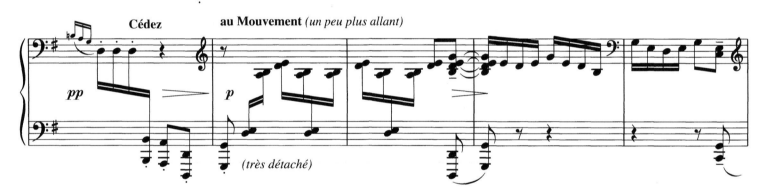

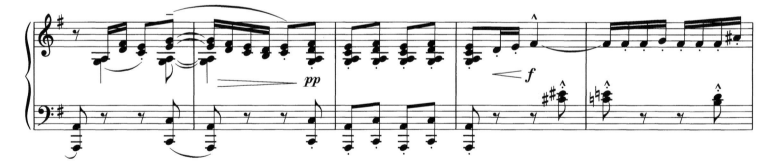

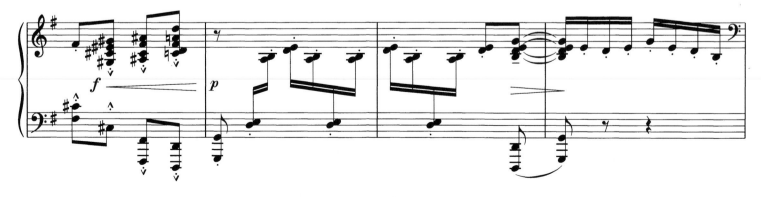

En cédant

au Mouvement

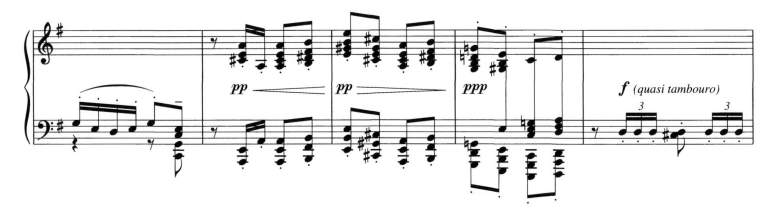

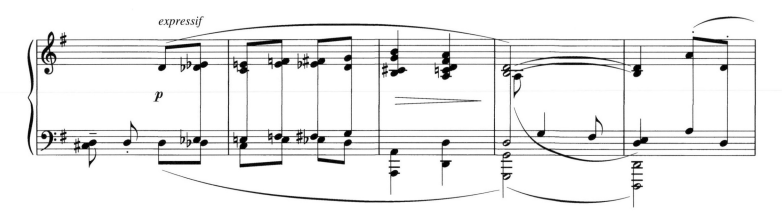

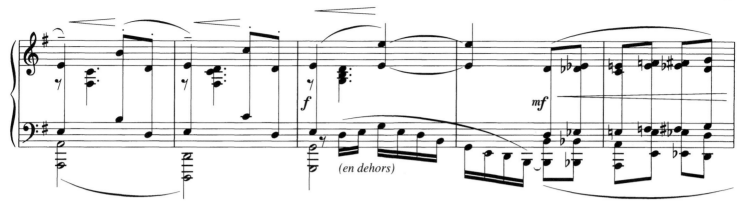

Tempo I

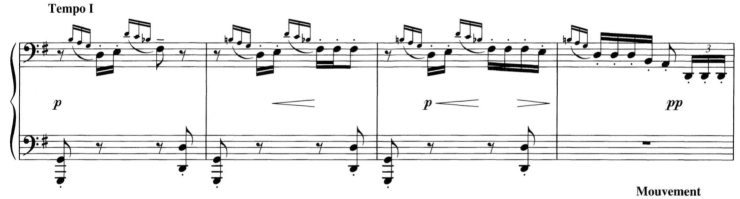

Mouvement
(plus allant)

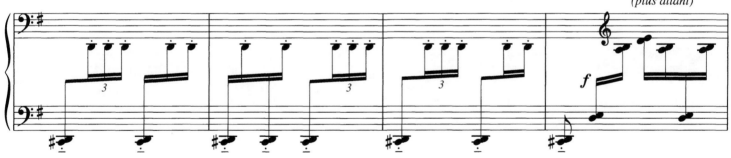

Serrez

Sec et retenu

La Cathédrale engloutie
(The Sunken Cathedral)

Claude Debussy
1862–1918

Profondément calme *(dans une brume doucement sonore)*

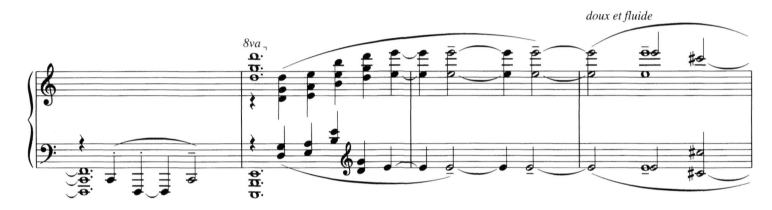

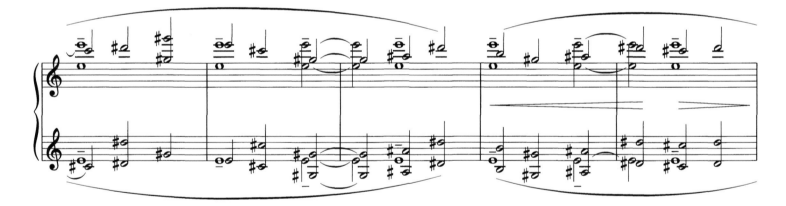

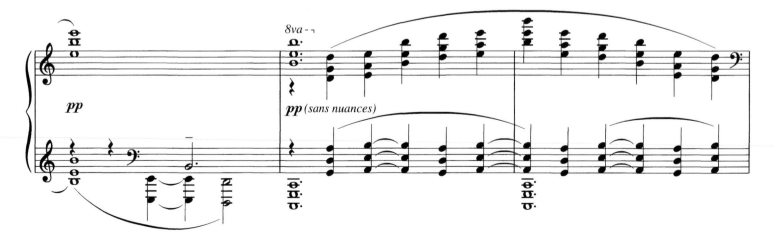

Peu à peu sortant de la brume

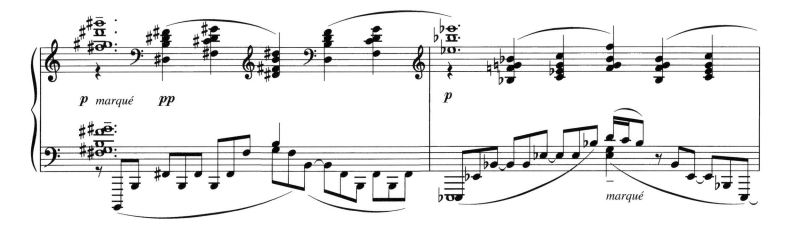

Augmentez progressivement *(sans presser)*

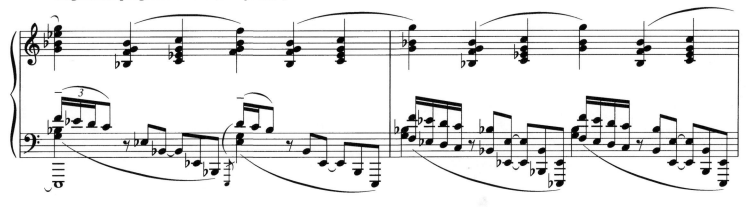

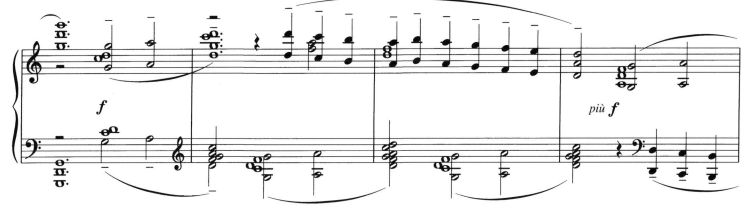

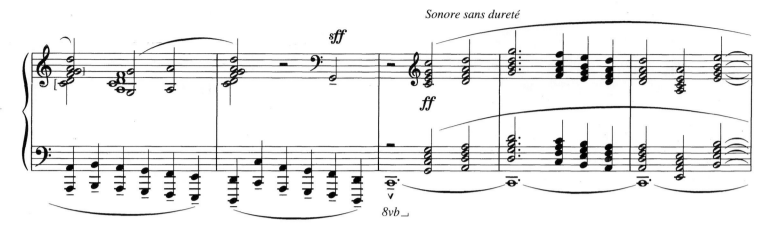

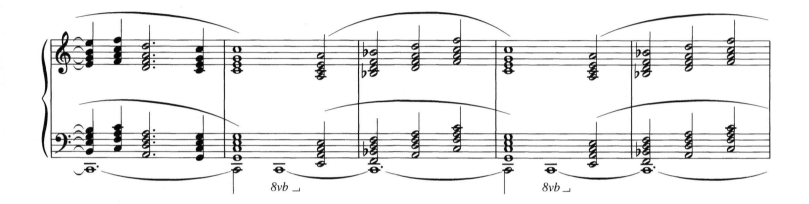

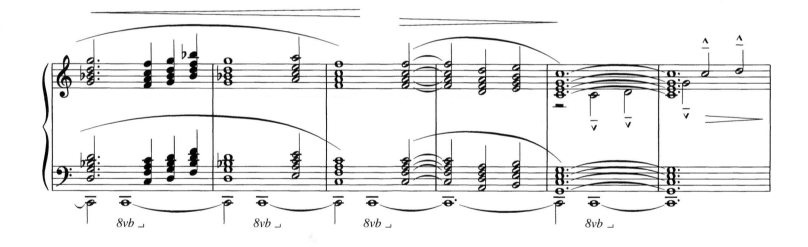

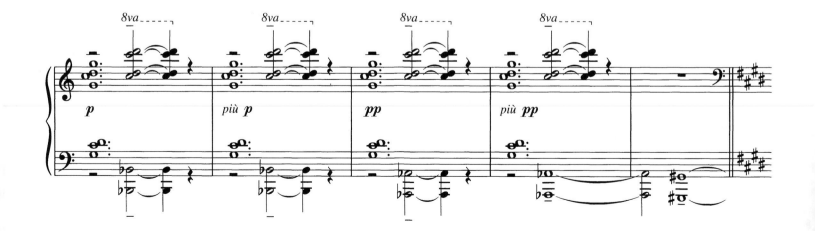

Un peu moins lent *(dans une expression allant grandissant)*

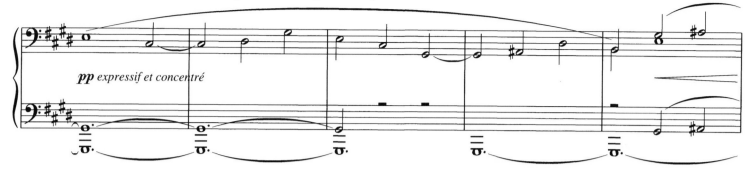

pp expressif et concentré

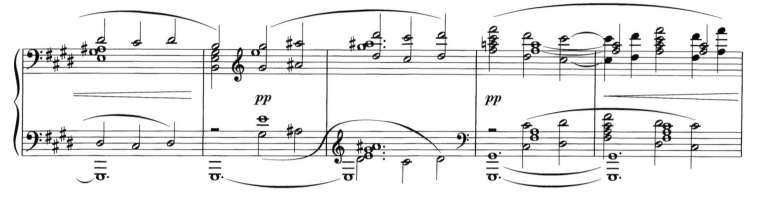

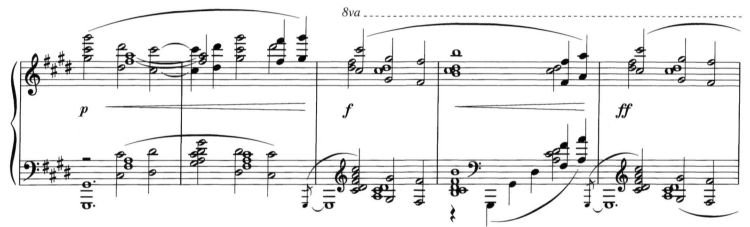

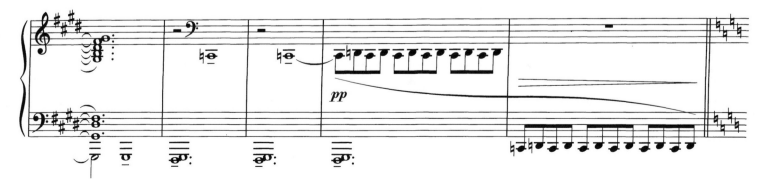

au Mouvement

pp comme un écho de la phrase entendue précédemment

Flottant et sourd.
8vb

(8vb)

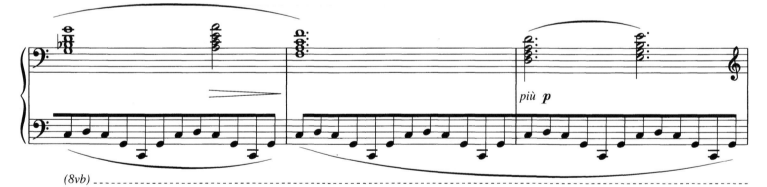

(8vb)

più *p*

Dans la sonorité du début

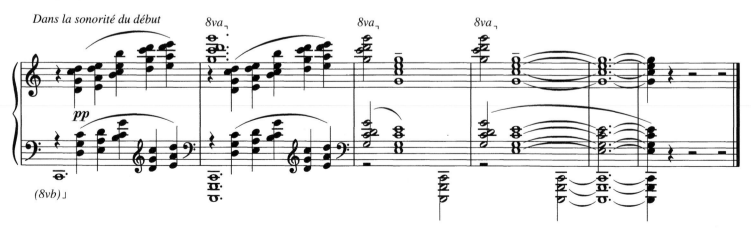

pp

(8vb)

To Spring
from LYRIC PIECES, BOOK 3

Edvard Grieg
1843–1907
Op. 43, No. 6

Allegro appassionato

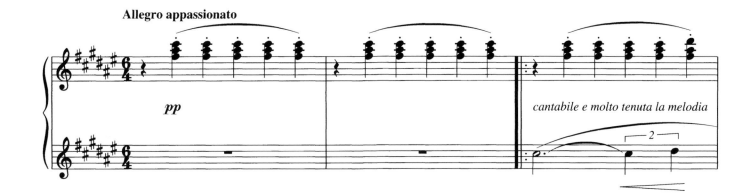

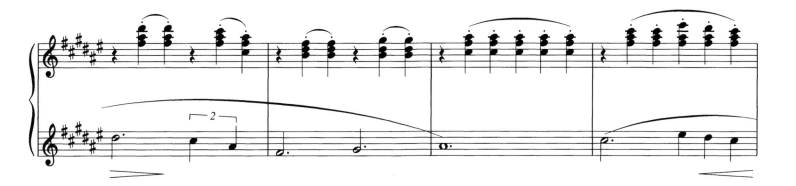

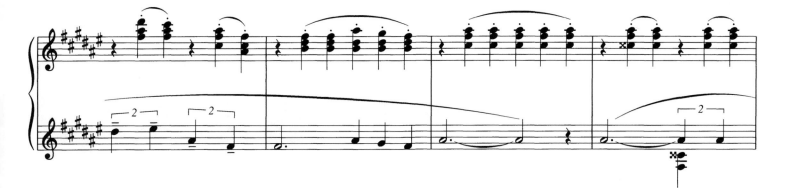

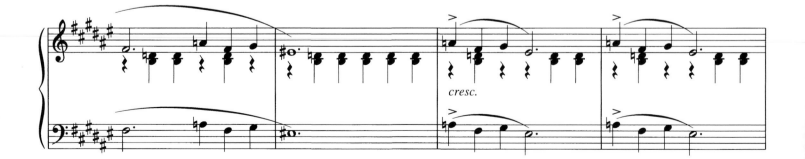

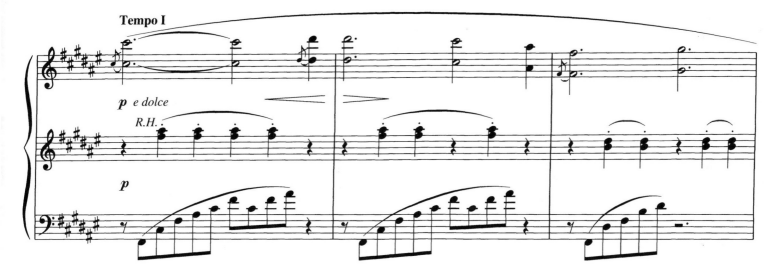

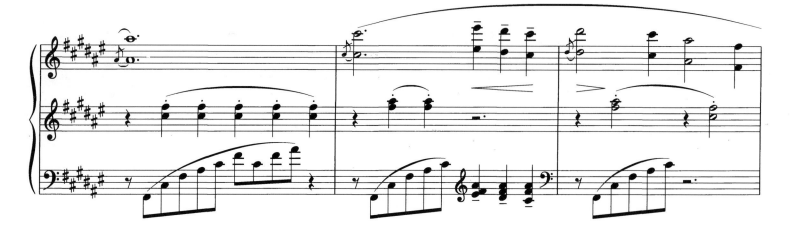

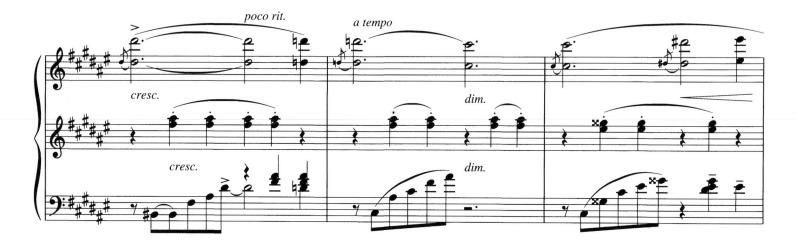

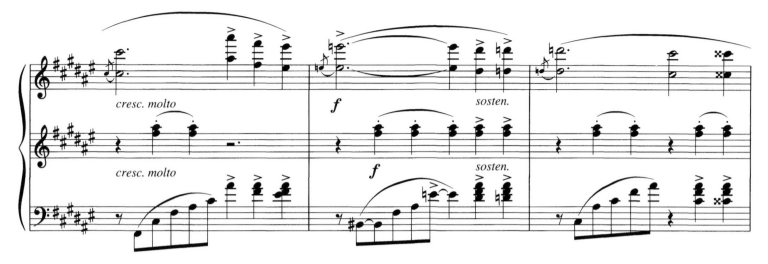

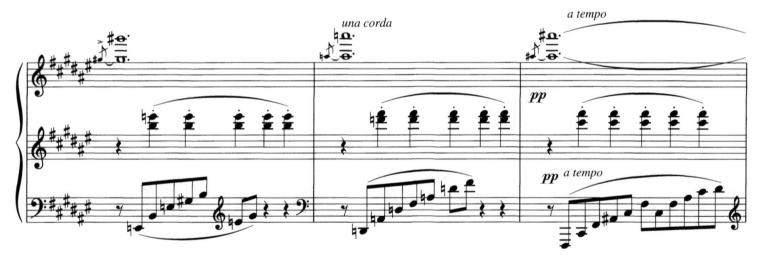

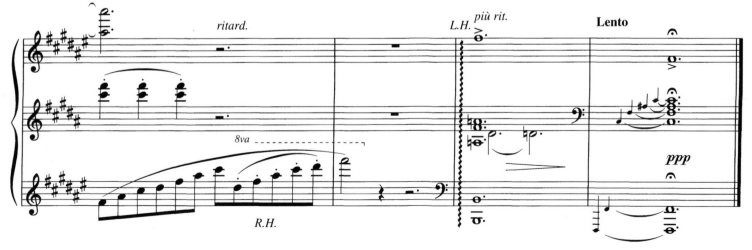

Spanish Dance No. 5
("Playera")

Enrique Granados
1867–1916

Andantino, quasi Allegretto

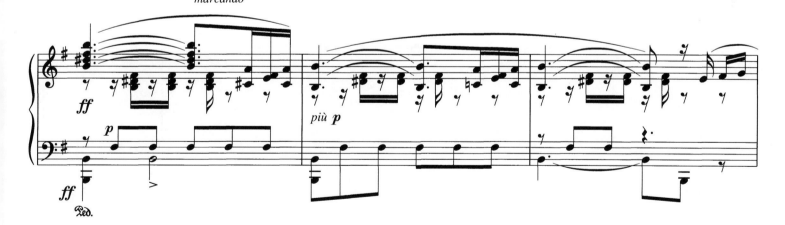

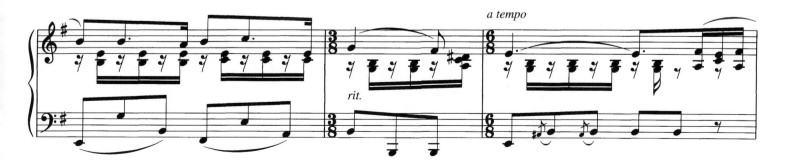

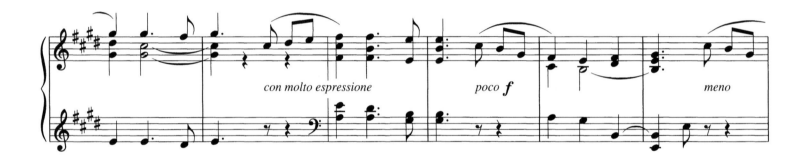

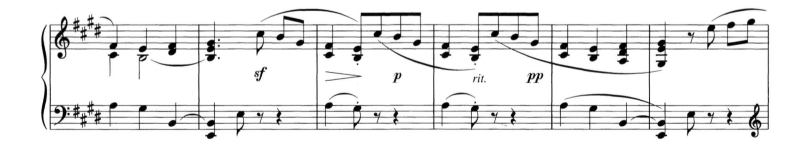

poco più mosso   meno   rit.

Andante molto

molto rit. e dim.

Tempo I

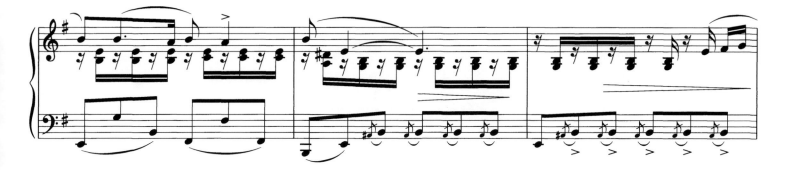

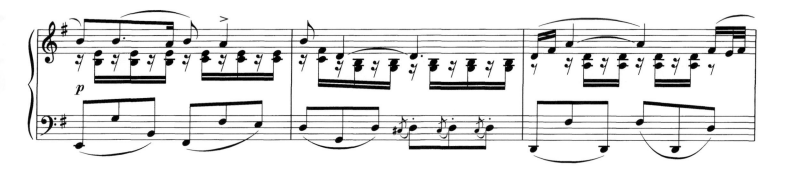

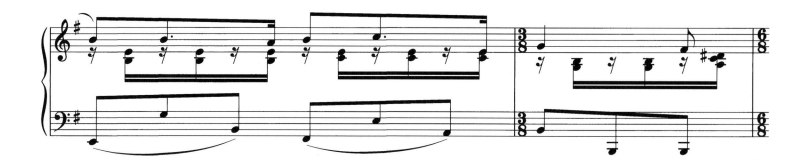

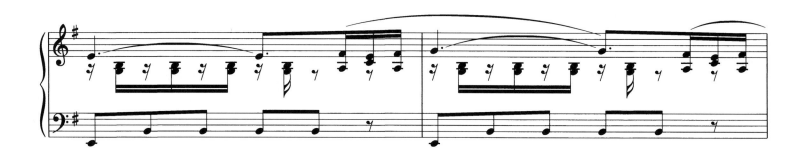

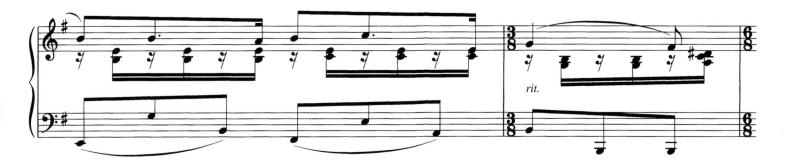

The White Peacock
from ROMAN SKETCHES

Charles Tomlinson Griffes
1884–1920
Op. 7, No. 1

Languidamente e molto rubato

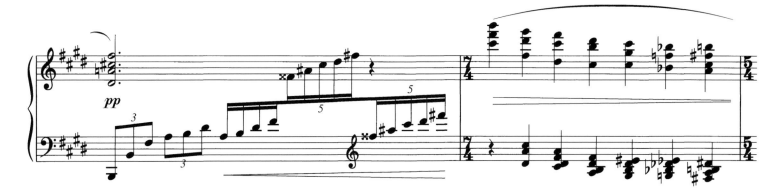

Con languore

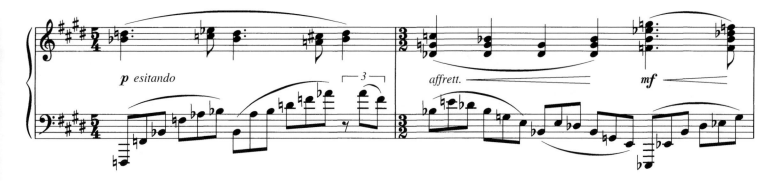

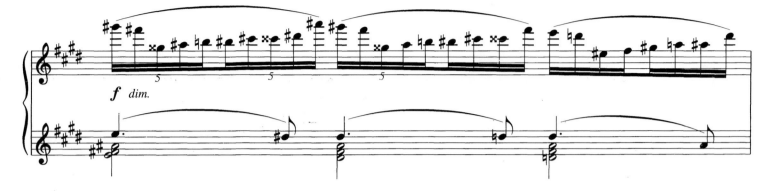

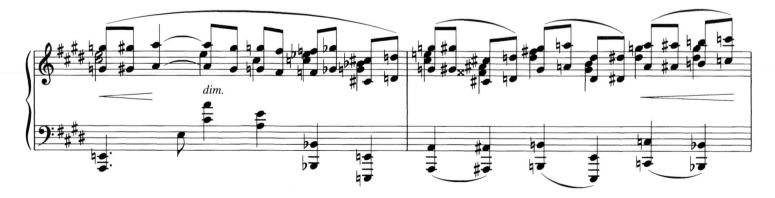

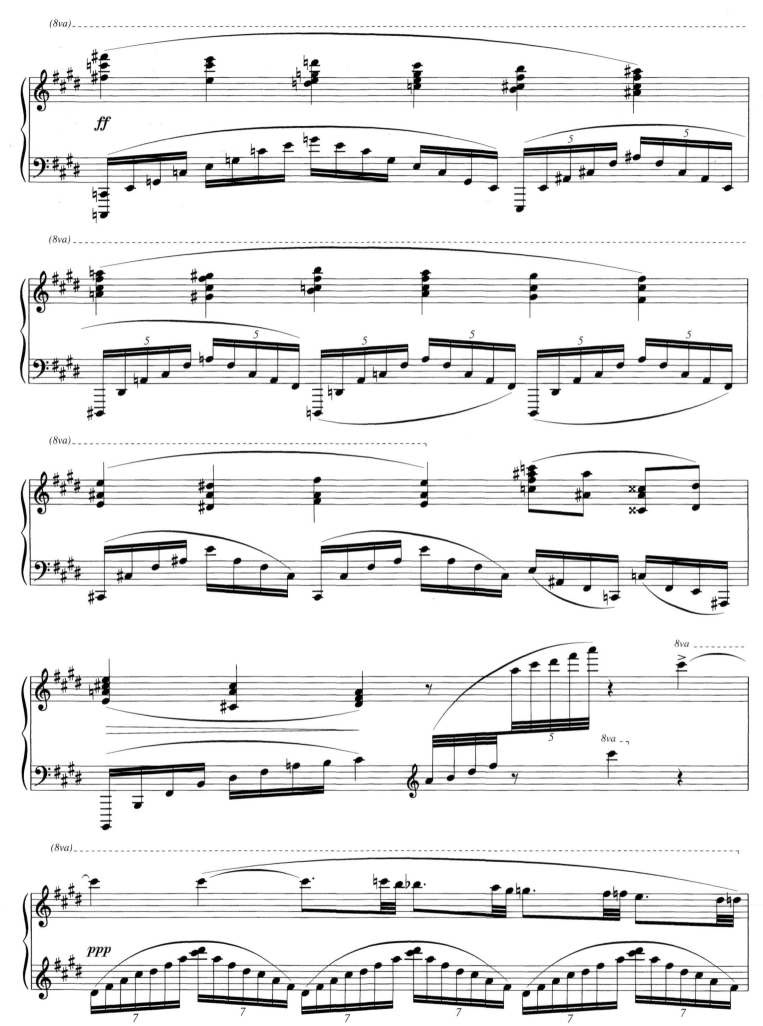

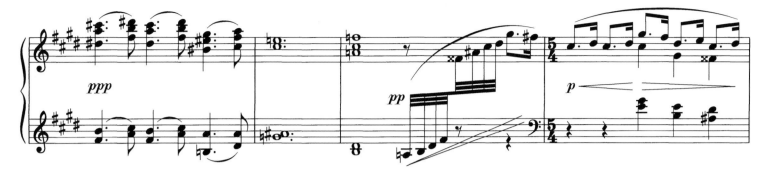

The Lake at Evening

Charles Tomlinson Griffes
1884–1920
Op. 5, No. 1

Tranquillo e dolce

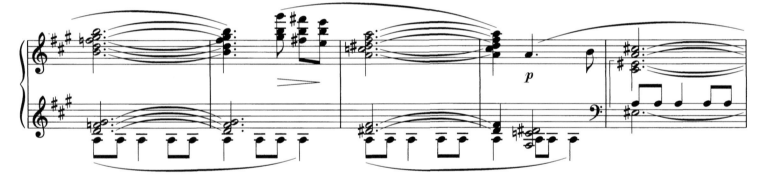

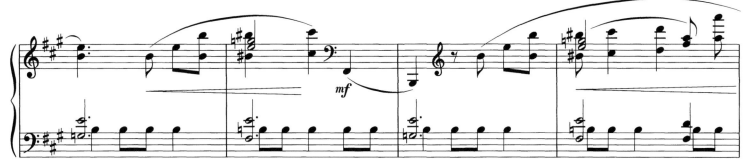

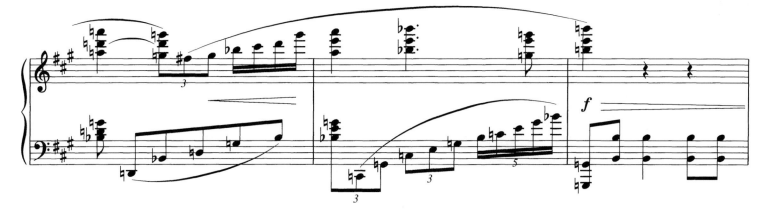

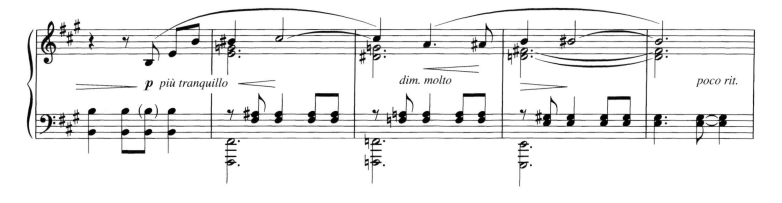

Tempo I

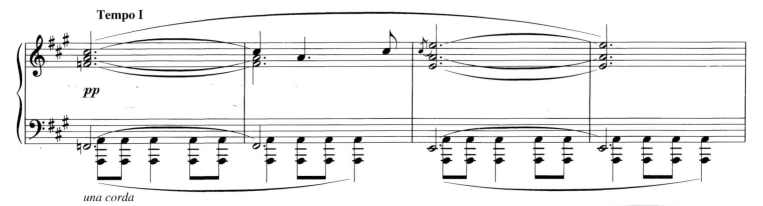

una corda

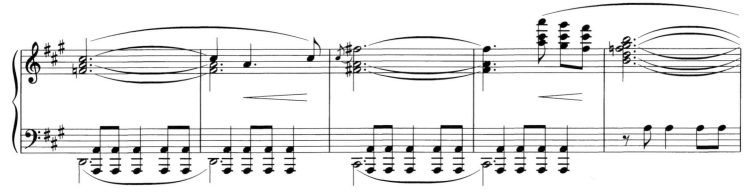

sempre dim. e più calmato

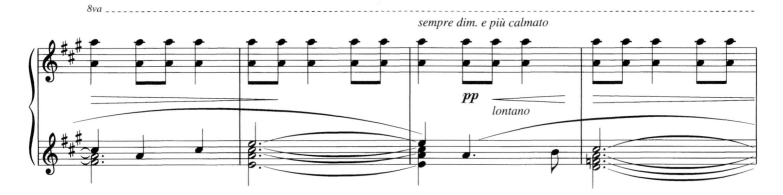

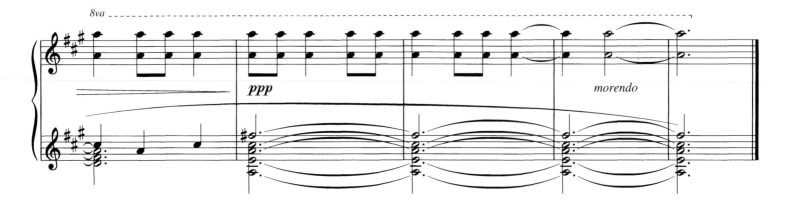

Liebestraum No. 3 in A-flat Major
(Nocturne No. 3)

Franz Liszt
1811–1886

Poco allegro, con affetto

dolce cantando

ten.

poco cresc. ed agitato

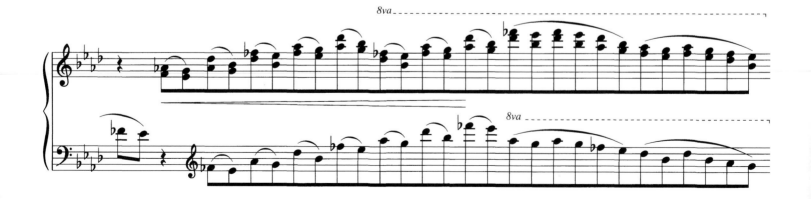

più animato, con passione

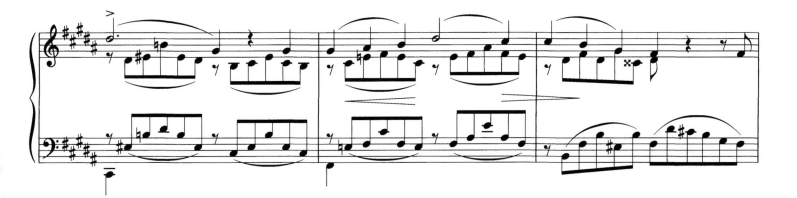

cresc.

sempre string.

f

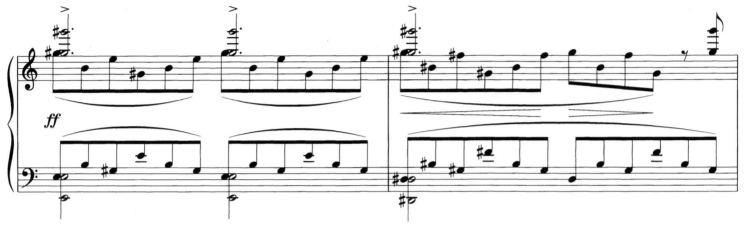

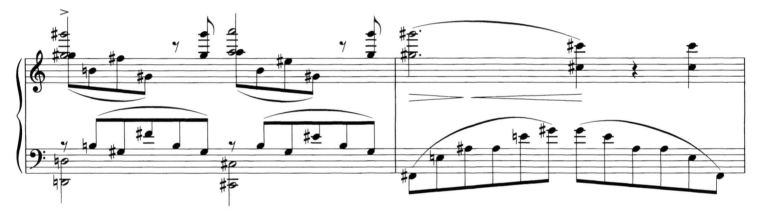

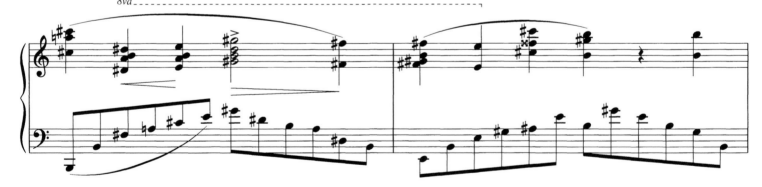

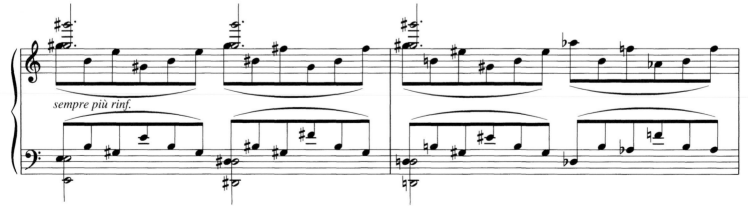

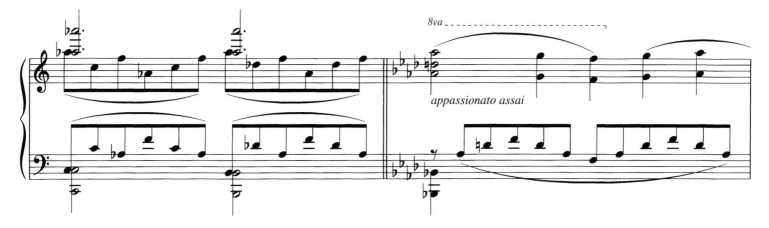

appassionato assai

rinforz.

affrett.

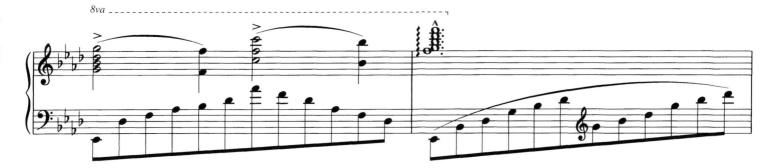

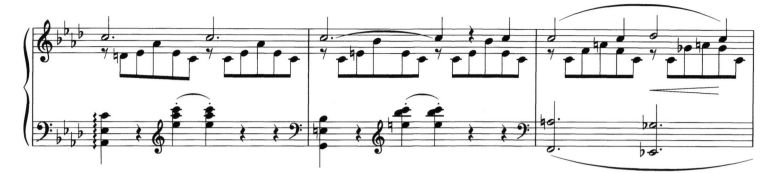

poco a poco riten.

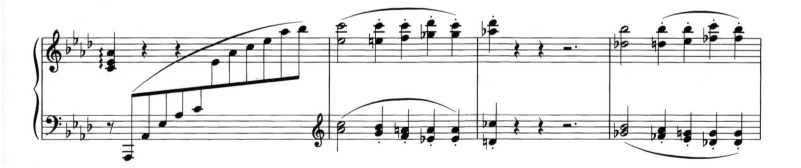

più smorz. e rit.

Solace
A Mexican Serenade

Scott Joplin
1868–1917

Very slow march time

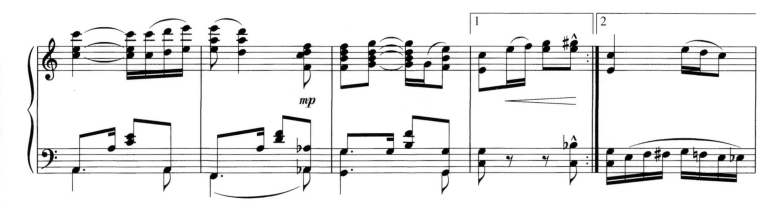

Spinning Song
from SONGS WITHOUT WORDS

Felix Mendelssohn
1809–1847
Op. 67, No. 4

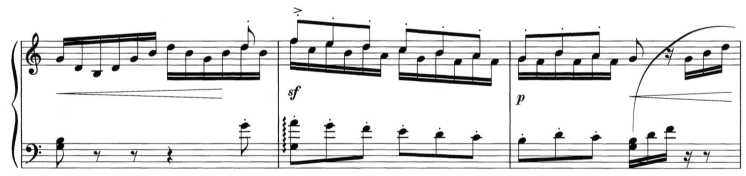

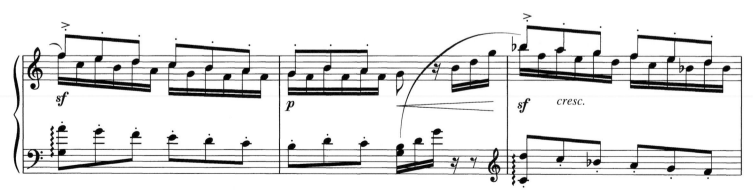

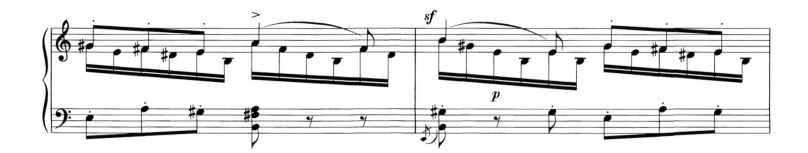

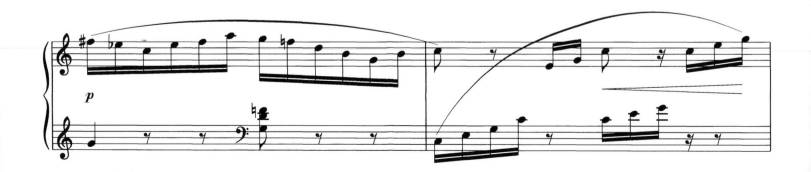

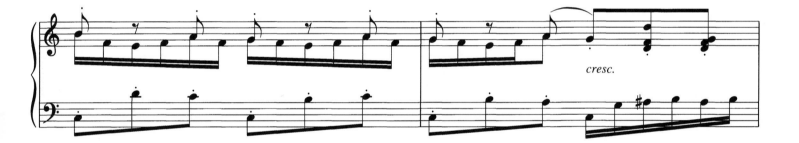

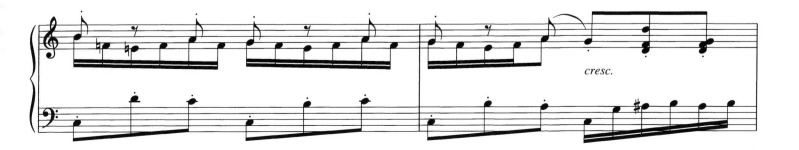

Rondo alla Turca
(Turkish Rondo)
from SONATA IN A MAJOR

Wolfgang Amadeus Mozart
1756–1791
K 331

Alla Turca

Allegretto

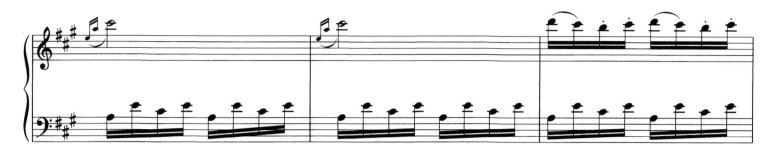

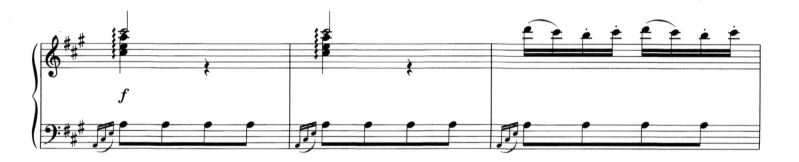

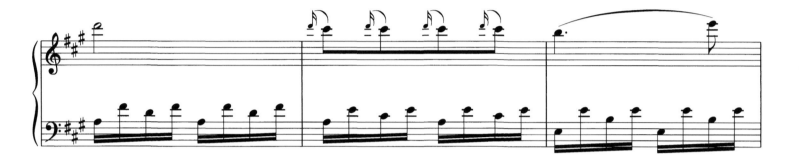

Rondo in D Major

Wolfgang Amadeus Mozart
1756–1791
K 485

Allegro

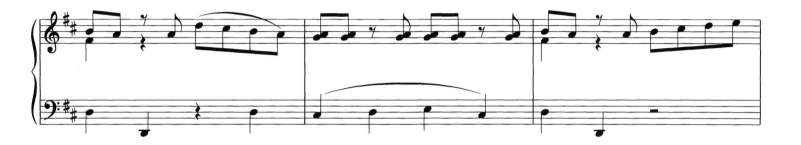

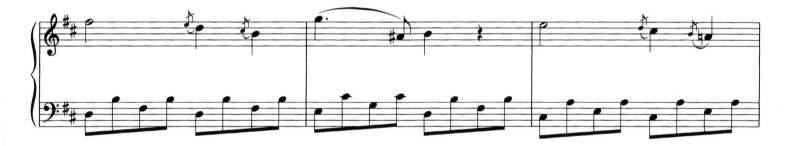

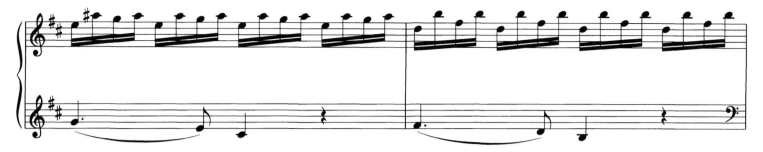

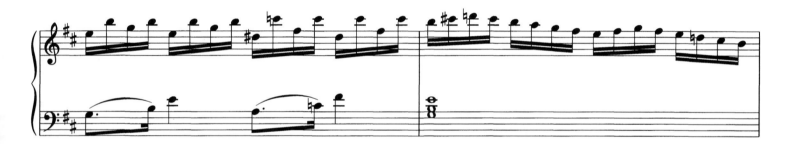

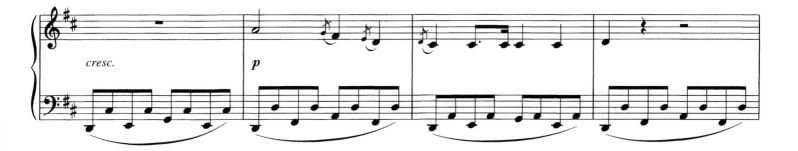

Menuet célèbre
from HUMORESQUES DE CONCERT

Ignacy Jan Paderewski
1860–1941
Op. 14, No. 1

Allegretto

mp non legato

p

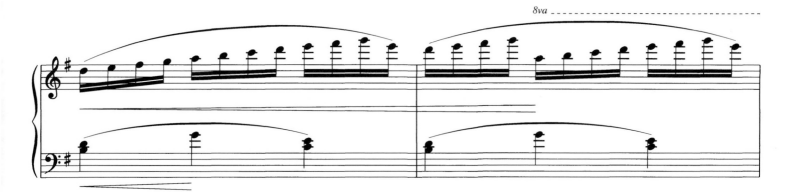

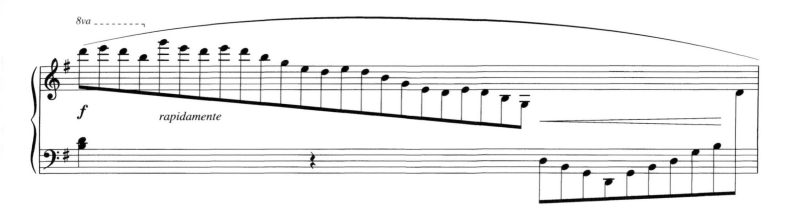

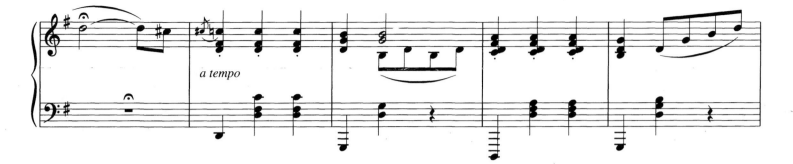

con forza la melodia

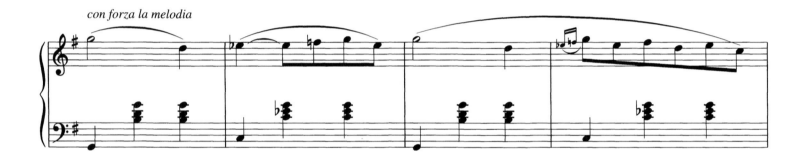

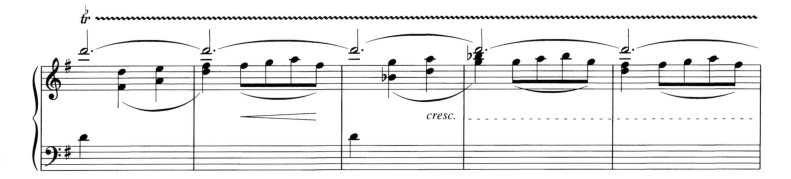

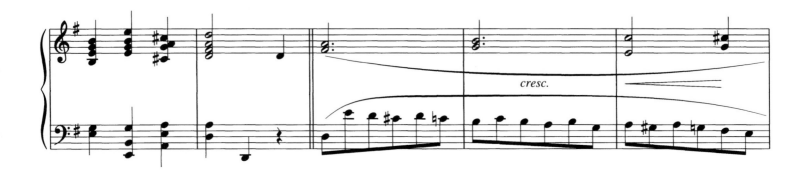

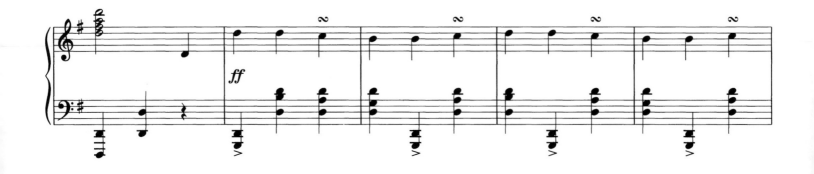

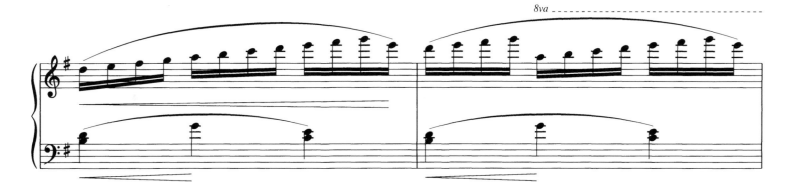

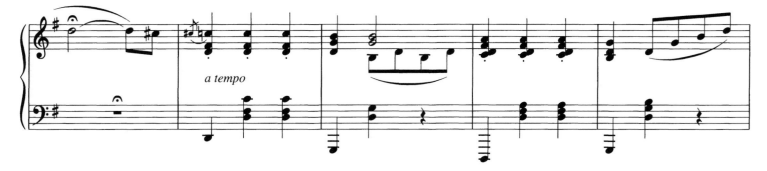

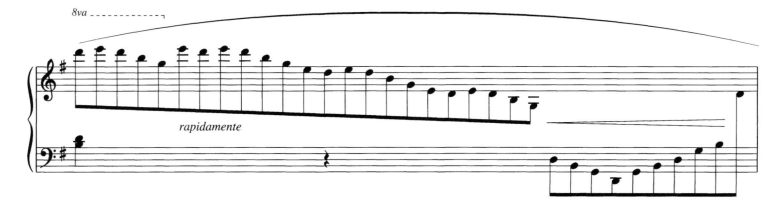

Coda
Vivo

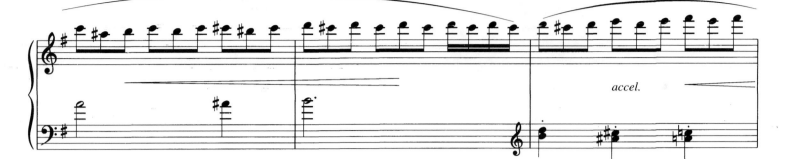

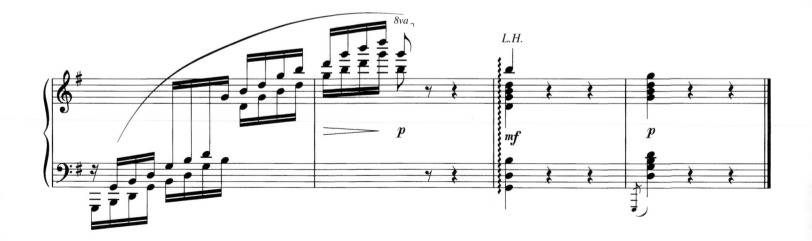

Prelude in G Minor

Sergei Rachmaninoff
1873–1943
Op. 23, No. 5

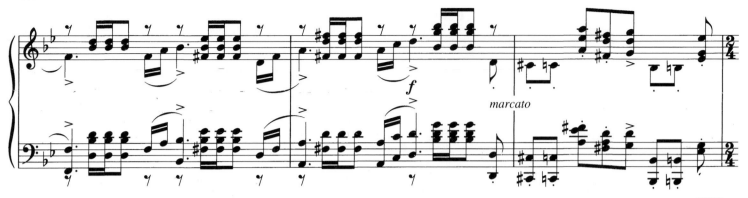

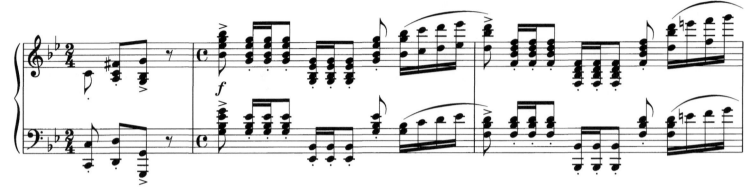

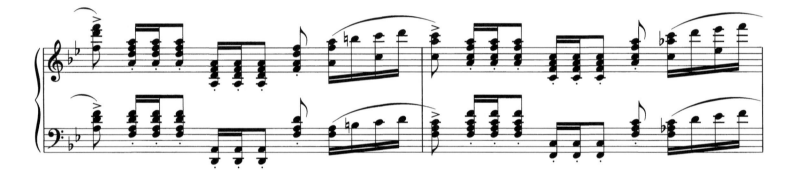

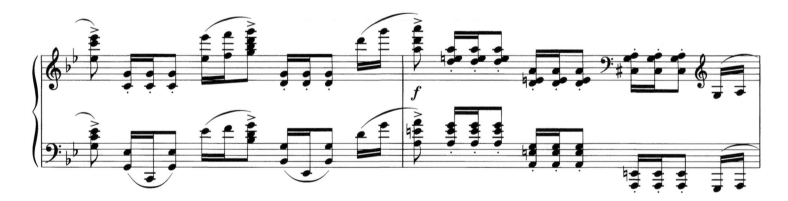

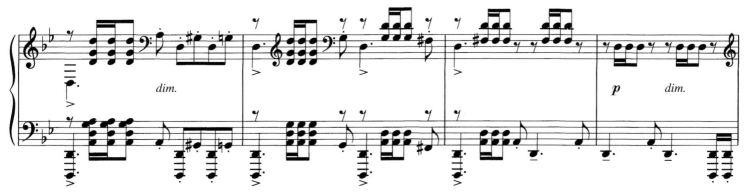

Un poco meno mosso

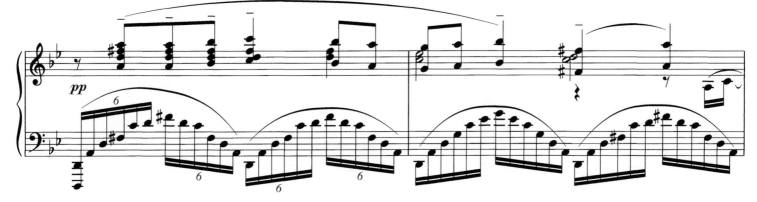

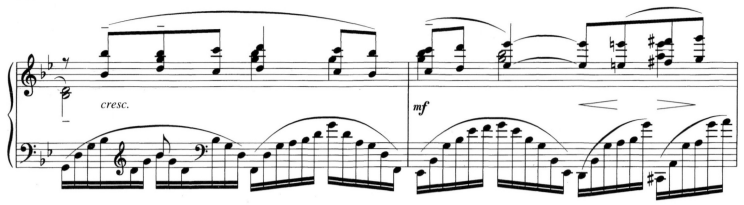

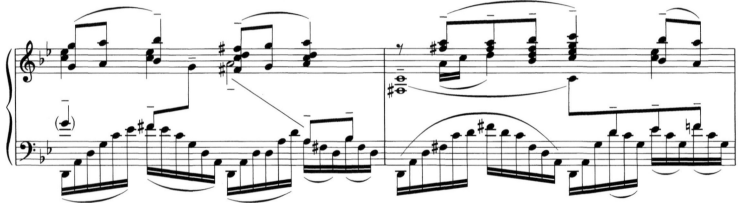

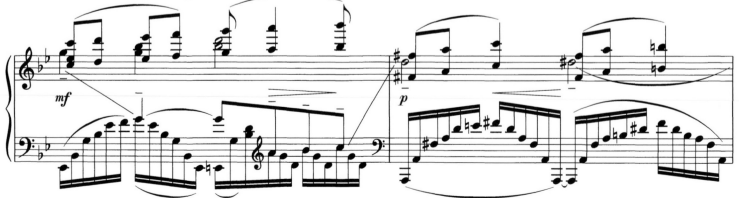

dim. e rit.

ppp

poco a poco accelerando e cresc. al Tempo I

Tempo I

f

cresc.

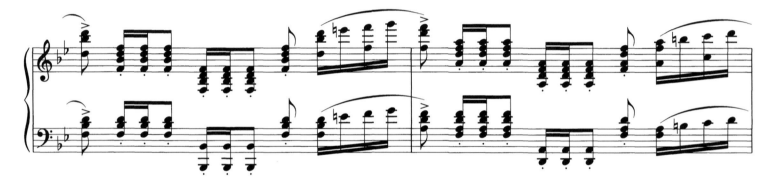

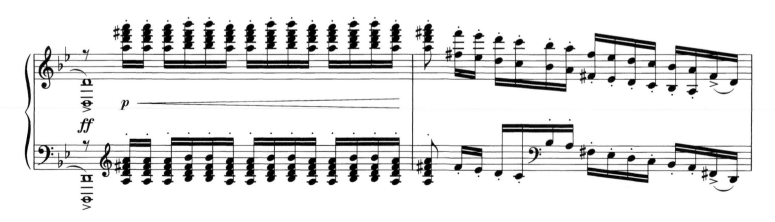

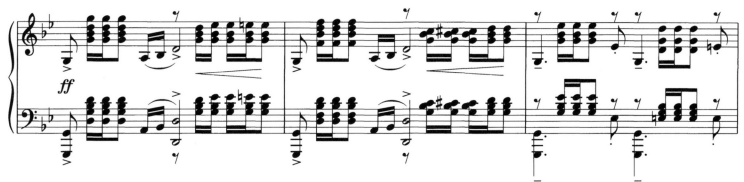

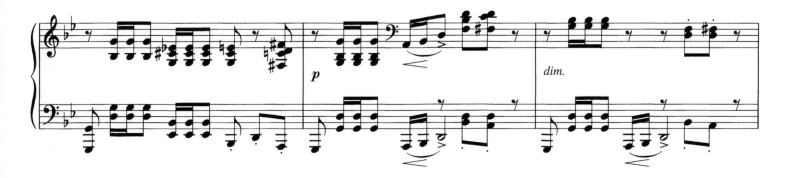

Prelude in D Major

Sergei Rachmaninoff
1873–1943
Op. 23, No. 4

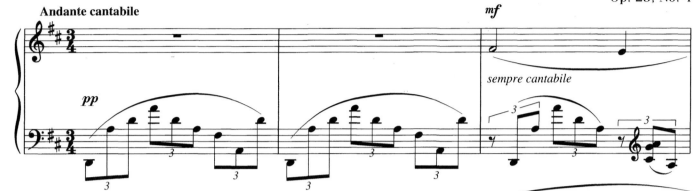

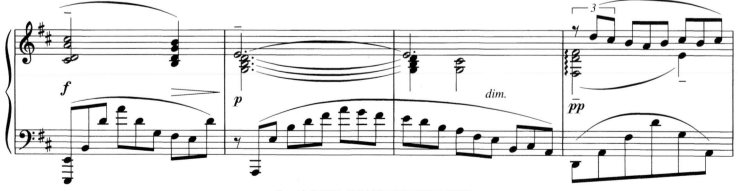

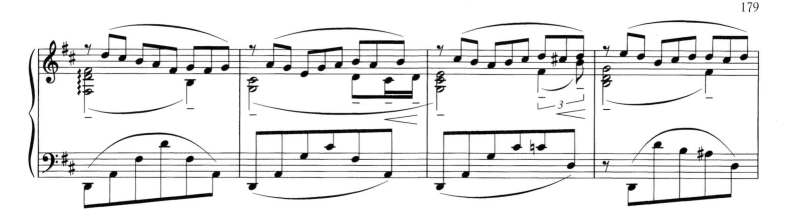

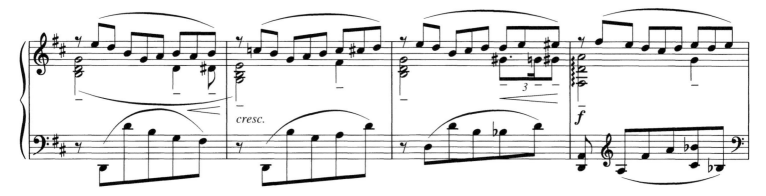

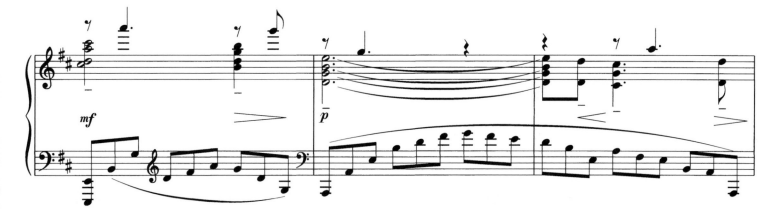

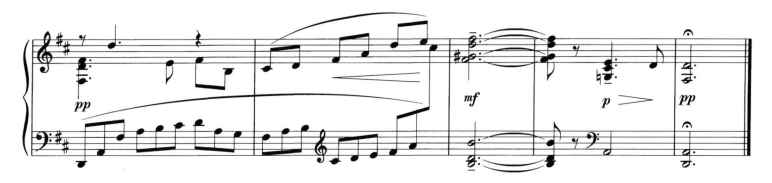

Prelude in G-sharp Minor

Sergei Rachmaninoff
1873–1943
Op. 32, No. 12

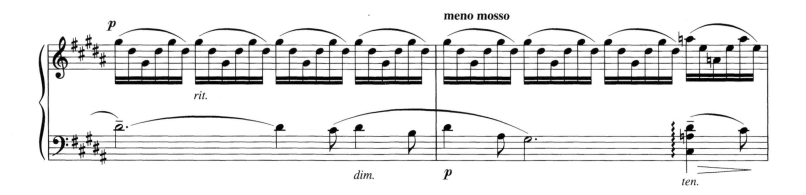

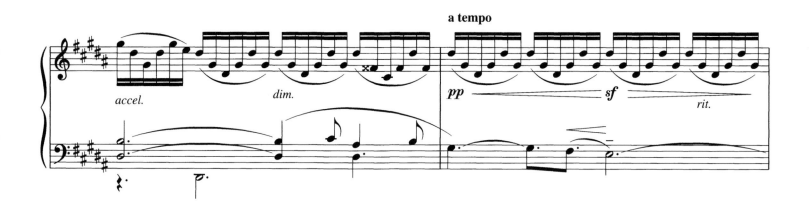

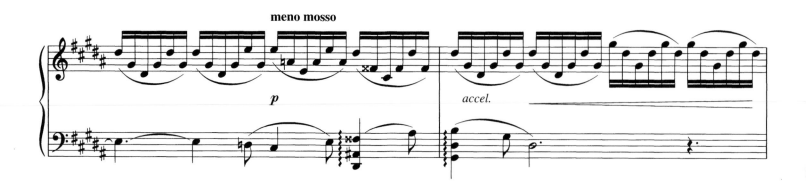

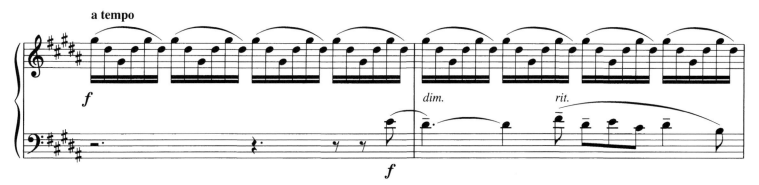

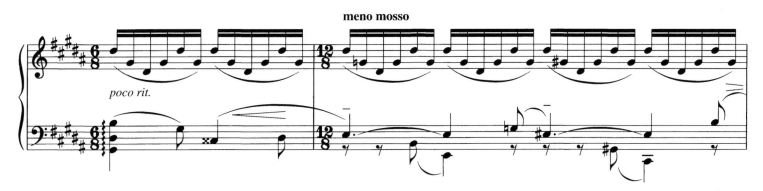

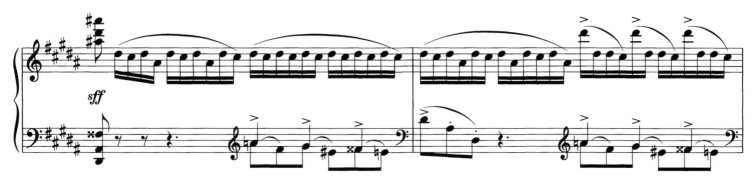

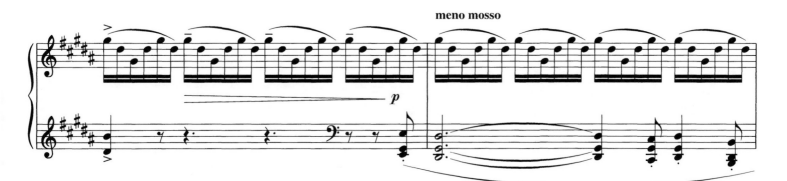

meno mosso

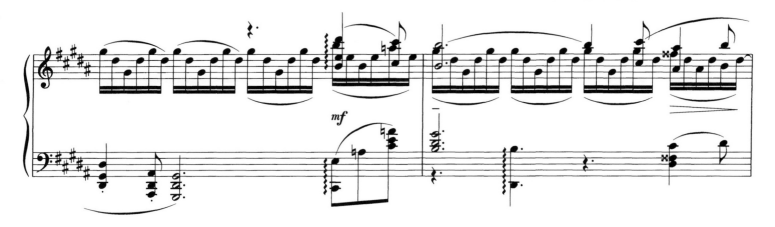

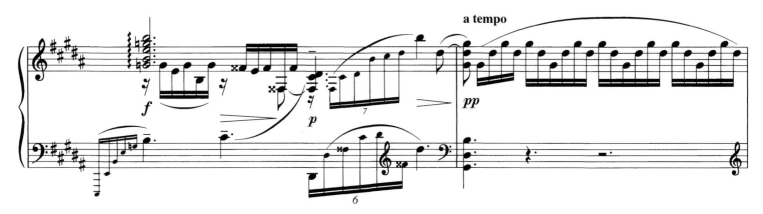

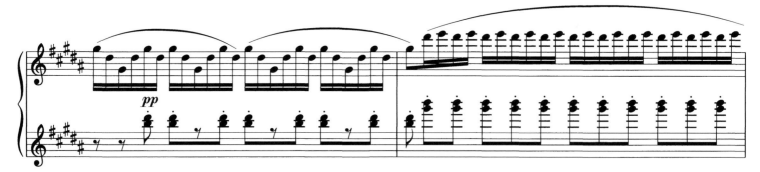

Melody in F Major

Anton Rubinstein
1829–1894
Op. 3, No. 1

Moderato

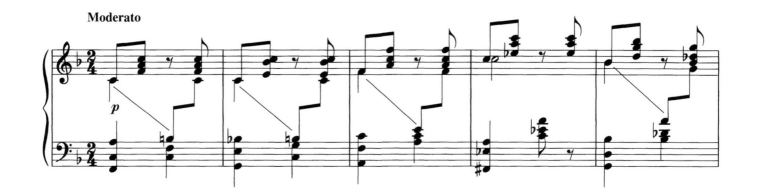

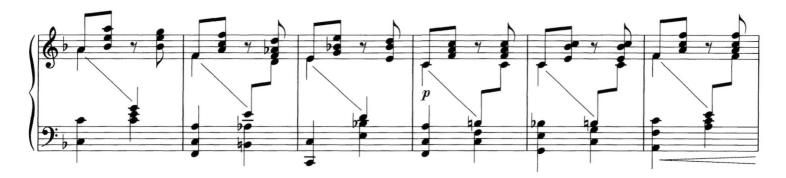

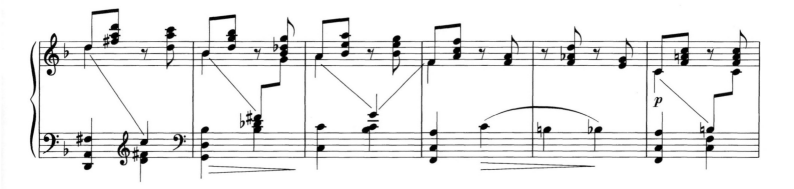

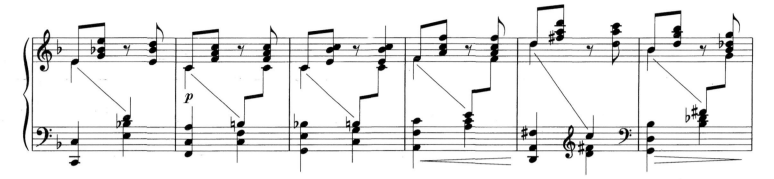

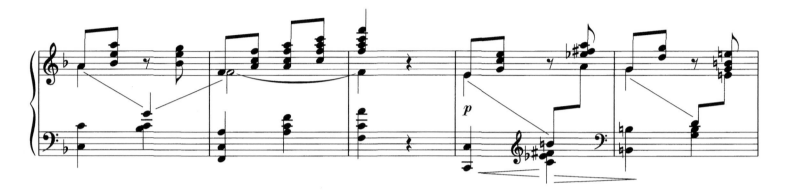

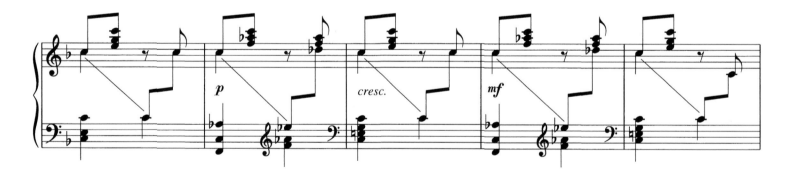

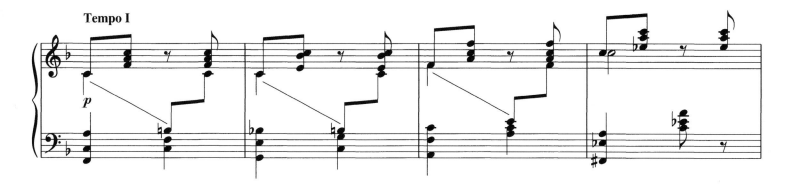

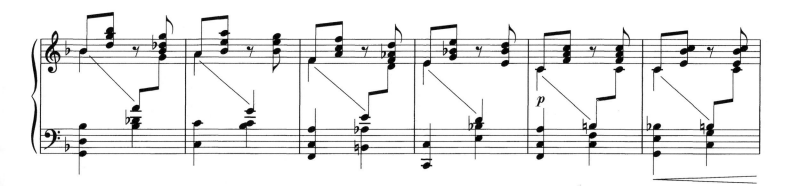

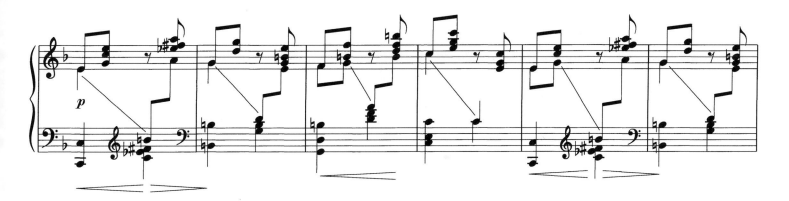

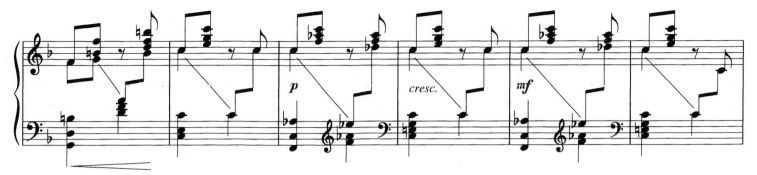

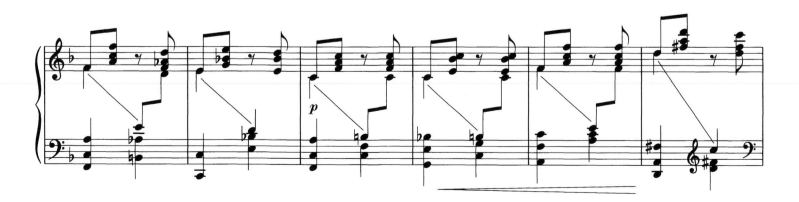

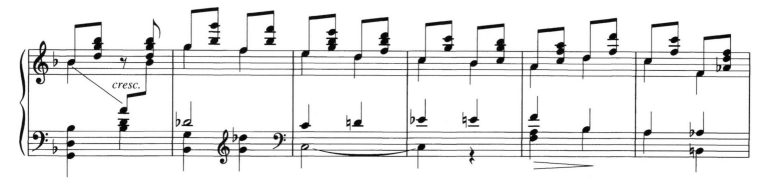

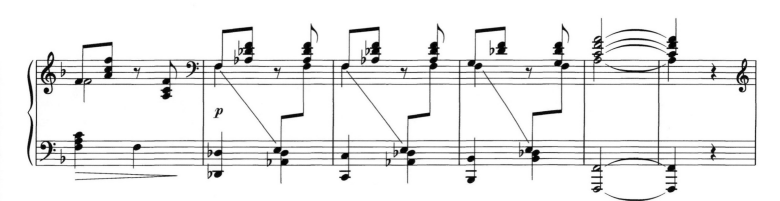

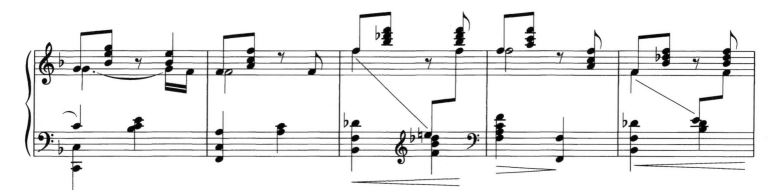

Romance in E-flat Major

Anton Rubinstein
1829–1894
Op. 44, No. 1

Andante con moto

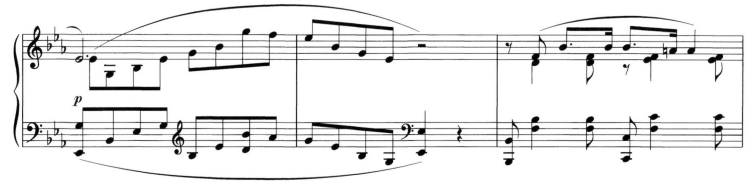

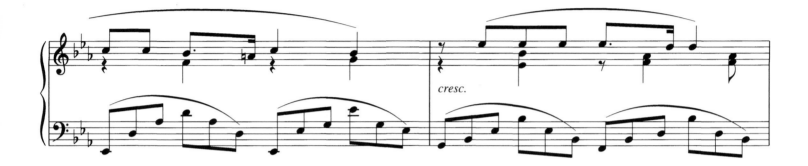

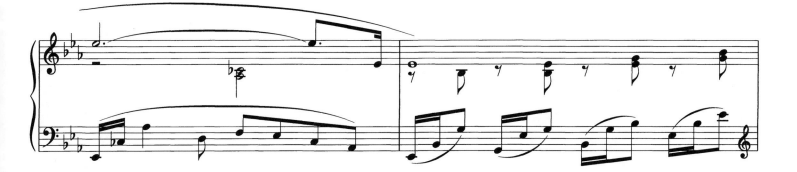

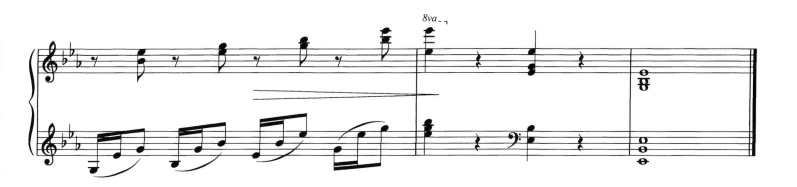

Pavane pour une infante défunte

Maurice Ravel
1875-1937

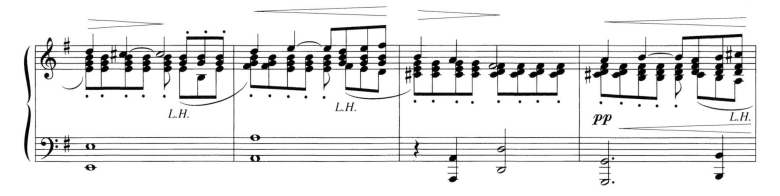

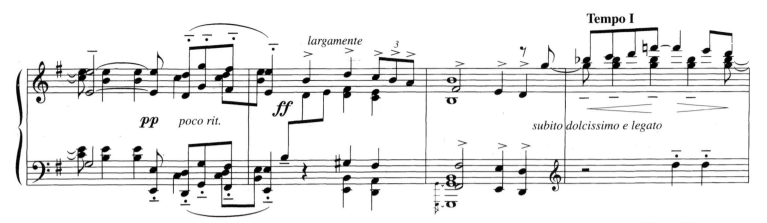

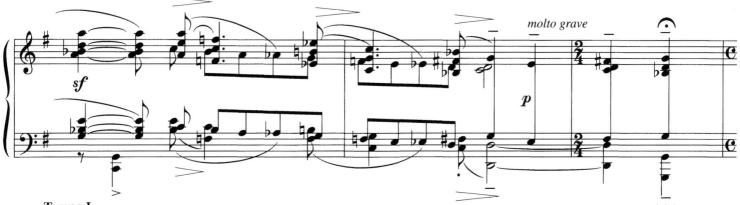

Tempo I

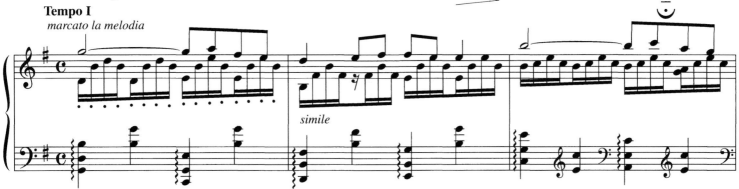

Rigaudon
from LE TOMBEAU DE COUPERIN

Maurice Ravel
1875–1937

Les petites notes doivent être frappées sur le temps.

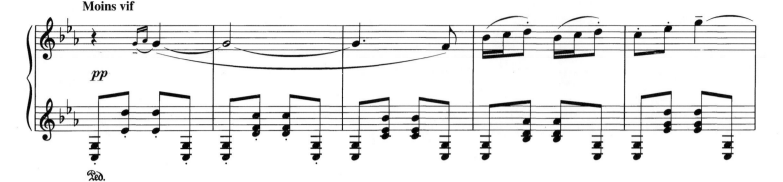

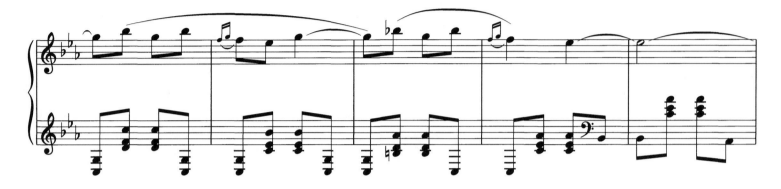

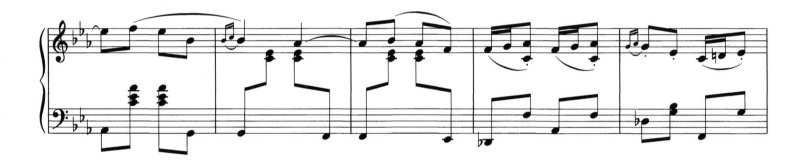

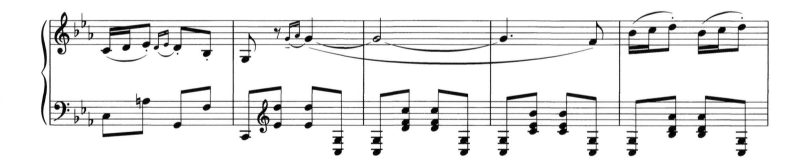

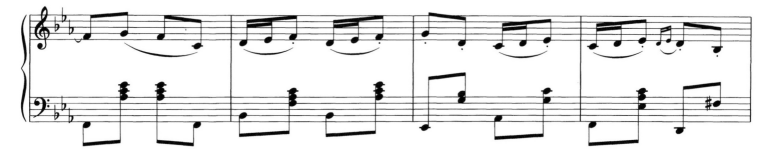

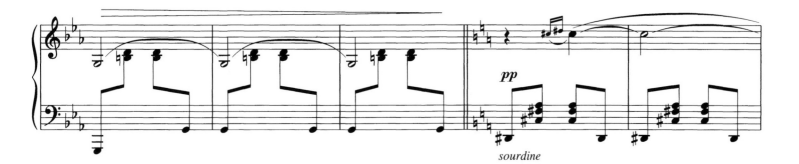

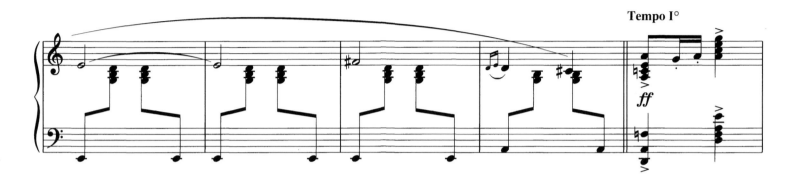

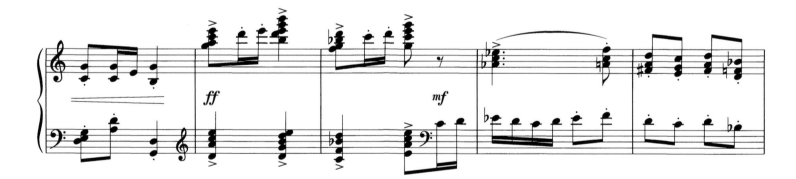

Sonata in E Major

Domenico Scarlatti
1685–1757
Longo 470 (K. 403, P. 437)

Sonata in E Minor

Domenico Scarlatti
1685–1757
Longo 427 (K. 402, P. 496)

Andante

Moment Musicale in F Minor

Franz Schubert
1797–1828
D. 780, No. 5 (Op. 94, No. 5)

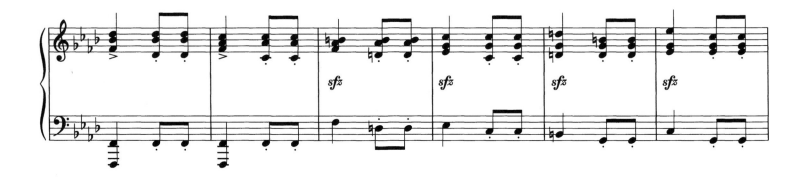

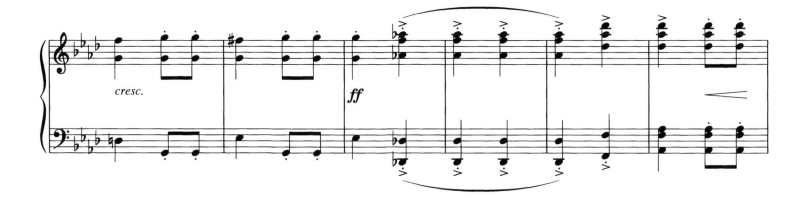

Moment Musicale in A-flat Major

Franz Schubert
1797–1828
D. 780, No. 2 (Op. 94, No. 2)

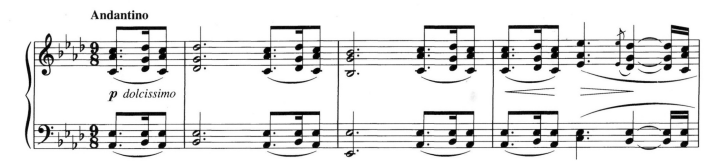

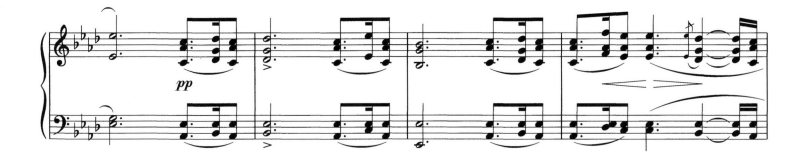

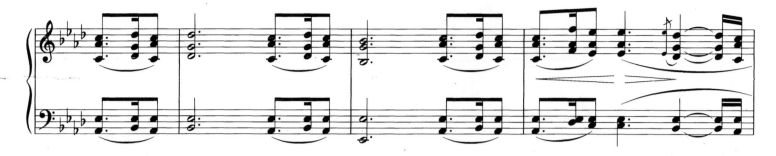

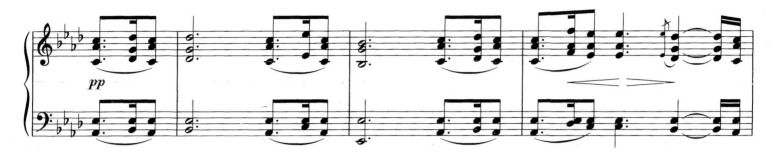

Etude in C-sharp Minor

Alexander Skryabin
1872–1915
Op. 2, No. 1

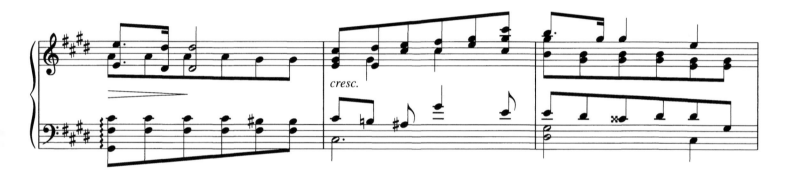

Etude in F-sharp Major
("The Mosquito")

Alexander Skryabin
1872–1915
Op. 42, No. 3

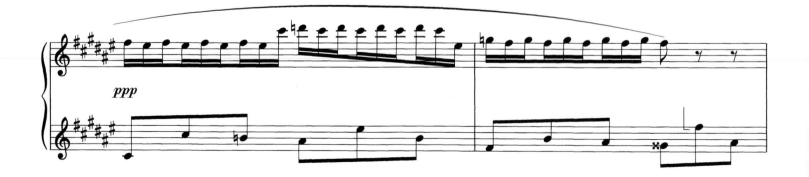

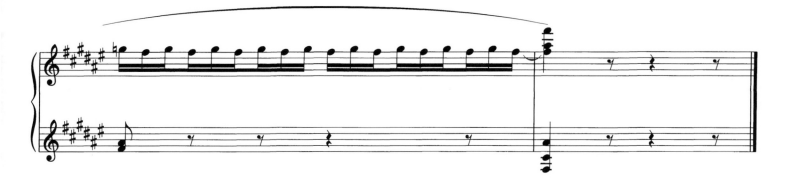

Arabesque

Robert Schumann
1810–1856
Op. 18

Leicht und zart

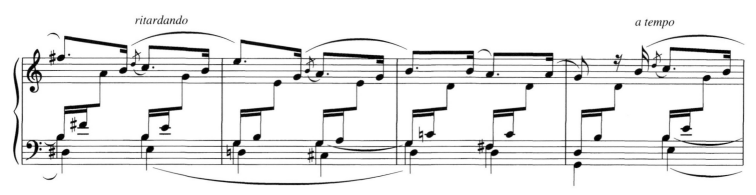

ritardando   *a tempo*

ritardando   *a tempo*

Minore I

Etwas langsamer

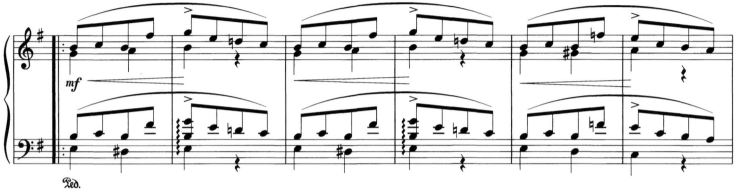

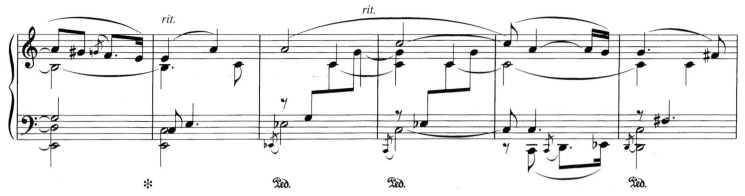

ritardando

a tempo　　　　　　　　　　　　　　　　　　　*rit.*

a tempo

Minore II
Etwas langsamer

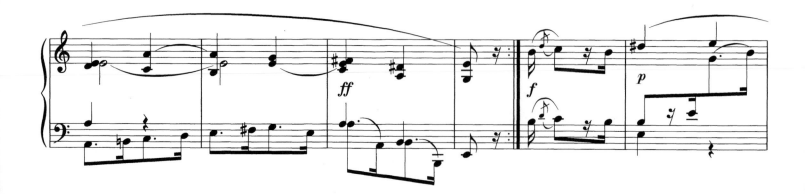

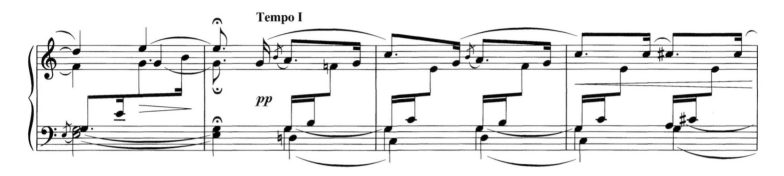

240

Zum Schluss
Langsam

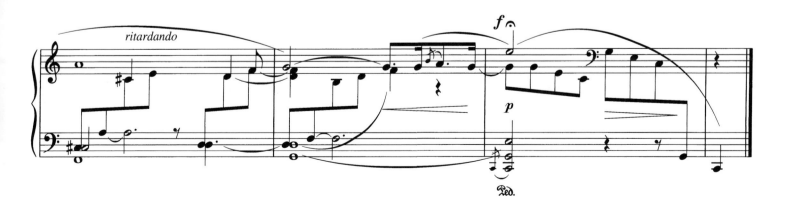

Barcarolle in G Minor (June)
from THE SEASONS

Pyotr Il'yich Tchaikovsky
1840–1893
Op. 37, No. 6

Andante cantabile

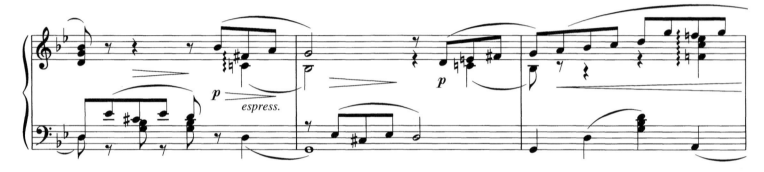

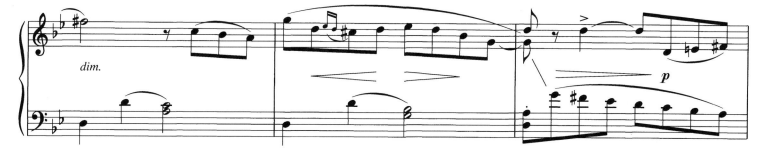

Poco più mosso

Allegro giocoso

Andante cantabile

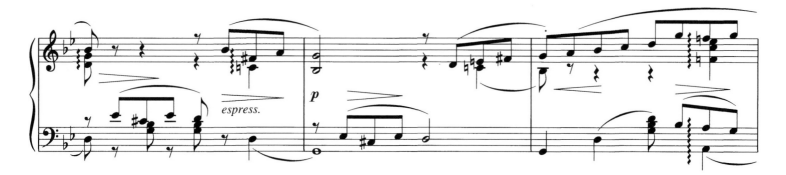

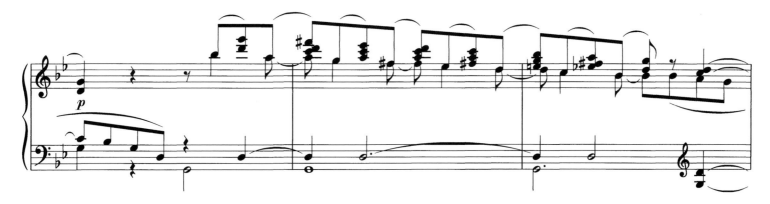

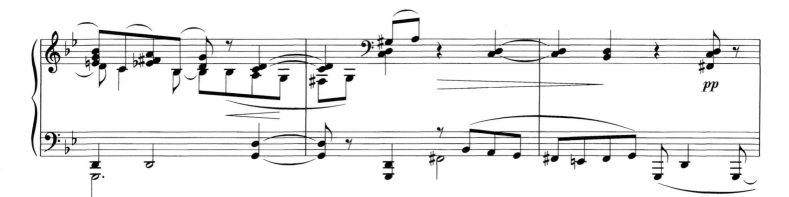

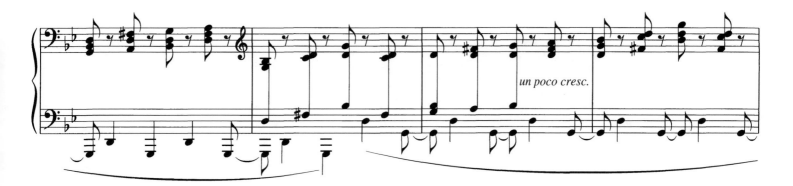

Chant sans paroles
from SOUVENIR DE HAPSAL

Pyotr Il'yich Tchaikovsky
1840–1893
Op. 2, No. 3

Allegretto grazioso e cantabile

Tempo I

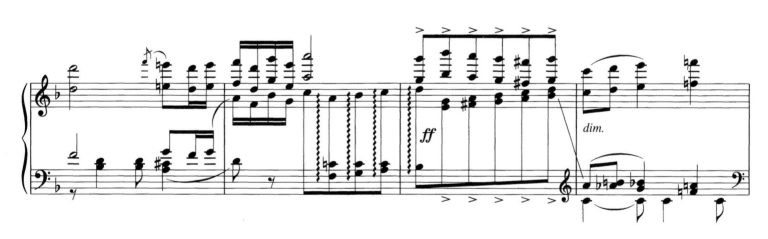

251

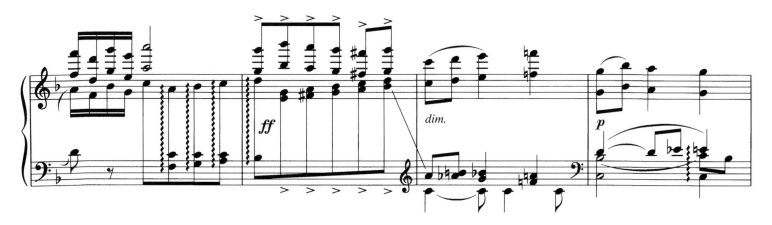

Humoresque
from DEUX MORCEAUX

Pyotr Il'yich Tchaikovsky
1840–1893
Op. 10, No. 2

Allegretto scherzando

Semplice, ma espress.

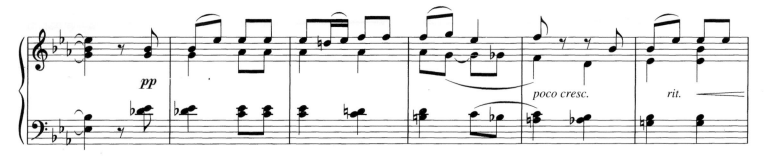

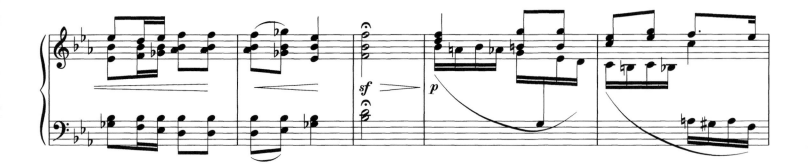

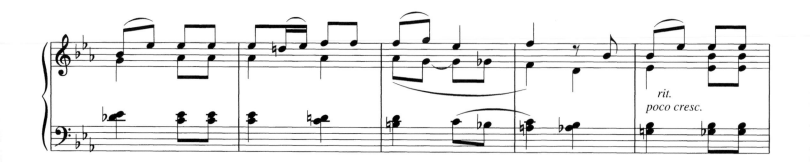

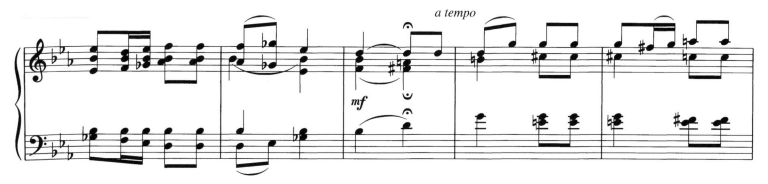

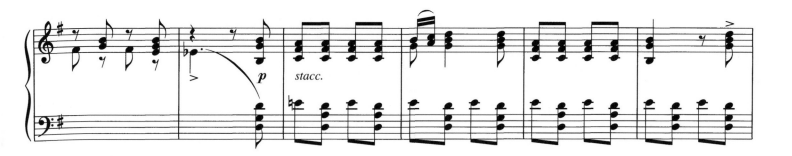

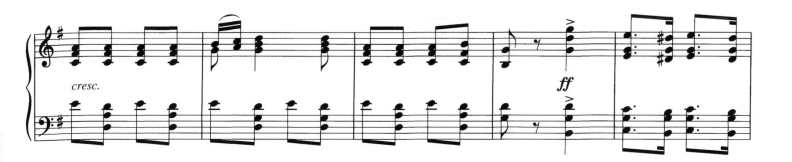

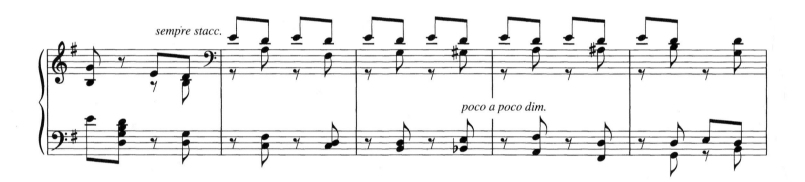

THE HORROR OF
WORLD WAR II

by Nancy Dickmann

Consultant: Philip Parker
Author and historian

capstone

Infosearch books are published by Capstone Press,
1710 Roe Crest Drive, North Mankato, Minnesota 56003
www.mycapstone.com

Library of Congress Cataloging-in-Publication Data
Library of Congress Cataloging-in-Publication data is available on the Library of Congress website.

978-1-4846-4165-1 (library binding)
978-1-4846-4169-9 (paperback)
978-1-4846-4173-6 (eBook PDF)

Editorial Credits
Editor: Nancy Dickmann
Designer: Rocket Design (East Anglia) Ltd
Production Specialist: Kathy McColley
Media Researchers: Nancy Dickmann,
Steve White-Thomson, and Izzi Howell
Illustrators: Rocket Design (East Anglia) Ltd and Ron Dixon

Photo Credits
Alamy: DOD Photo, 43, Everett Collection Historical, 6, 38, Granger Historical Picture Archive, 29, 30,
Nordicphotos, 28, Paul Broadbent, 33, RGB Ventures/SuperStock, 15, World History Archive, 34, 40, 42,
Shutterstock: Aksenenko Olga, 3 (dirt), 44 (dirt), Aleksandra Pikalova, 3 (grenade), chrisdorney, 26, Edvard
Molnar, 25 (soldier silhouette), Elzbieta Sekowska, 8, Everett Historical, 1, 4, 5, 7, 9, 11, 12, 14, 18, 20, 24,
25, 27, 31, 32, 35, 36, 37, 41, Jorg Hackemann, 17, LandFox, 16, Leonard Zhukovsky, 23, Martial Red, 7
(skull and crossbones), Oliver Denker, 13, pkorchagina, 19, Tshooter, 15 (warship outlines), SuperStock:
cover, Fototeca Gilardi/Marka, 22.

Printed in the United States of America.
010365F17

Table of Contents

What Was World War II?

The first truly global war lasted from 1914 to 1918. It was long and bloody and involved people from around the world. It was so destructive that many hoped it would be "the war to end wars" — but it wasn't. Just 20 years later, the world was plunged into an even bigger, deadlier war.

In September 1939, Germany invaded Poland. This set off a chain of events that would see dozens of countries pulled into the war. By the end, about 50 to 60 million people were dead. This was about 2.5 percent of the entire world population at the time. Well over half of the deaths were **civilians**, including many children.

■ Millions of civilians were killed or forced from their homes during the war.

TOTAL WAR

Powerful new weapons, such as **atomic bombs**, made WWII extremely deadly. But this wasn't just a war fought by soldiers. Civilians were deeply involved as well. Some made weapons and **ammunition**, while others filled in for workers who were away fighting. This involvement made them targets. Some were forced to work and others were killed outright. Bombing raids on cities targeted all civilians living there, not just those working for the war effort. Millions of people suffered food shortages as a result of the war.

We often use **primary sources** to learn about the past. A primary source is a document, photograph or artifact made during the time that is being studied. Soldiers' letters and diaries are primary sources. So are photographs taken during battles.

■ The fighting left roads and towns in ruins, making life difficult.

How Did the War Start?

World War II had its roots in World War I. In 1918, Germany and its allies had been defeated by a coalition of France, Russia, the United Kingdom, and the United States. After the war, the losers were treated harshly. Germany had to pay huge amounts of **compensation** to other countries. It lost some of its territory, and its military was restricted.

After WWI, **inflation** in Germany spiraled out of control. Money became so worthless that some people burned it for fuel.

A WORLD IN TURMOIL

The war had left the economies of many countries in ruins. A worldwide **depression** soon followed. In some countries, huge numbers of people were out of work and struggling to get by. This caused anger and unrest. People started to look for strong leaders to solve their countries' problems.

In some countries, powerful **dictators** took charge. They promised to make their nation great, no matter what it took. In Italy, Germany, and Spain, they turned to **fascism**. The idea of this extreme form of nationalism was to keep a particular country strong at all costs. The leaders of these countries didn't believe in **democracy**, and they crushed any opposition.

FATAL FACTS

In 1936, a civil war began in Spain. Parts of the military had launched a revolt against the left-wing government. Other countries, including Germany and the Soviet Union, got involved. The war lasted several years and killed at least 500,000 people. The war showed that peace in Europe was very shaky. It would not take much to set off another war.

FASCISM IN GERMANY

In Germany, a WWI veteran named Adolf Hitler was becoming popular. He became leader of the German Workers' Party in 1921. He renamed it the National Socialist German Workers' Party — or the Nazi Party, for short. In 1933, he was named **chancellor** of Germany. He soon had complete control of the country.

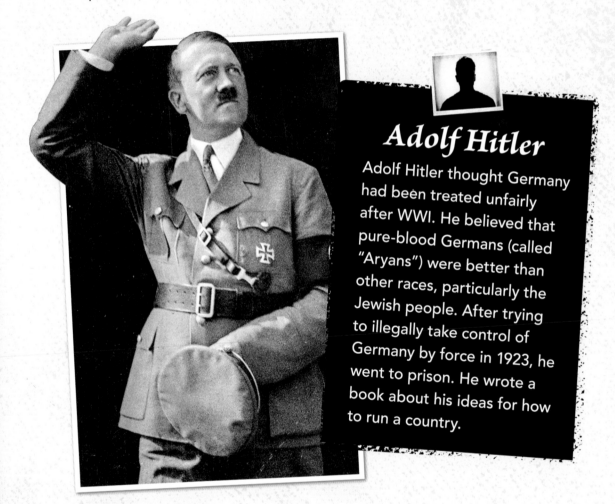

Adolf Hitler

Adolf Hitler thought Germany had been treated unfairly after WWI. He believed that pure-blood Germans (called "Aryans") were better than other races, particularly the Jewish people. After trying to illegally take control of Germany by force in 1923, he went to prison. He wrote a book about his ideas for how to run a country.

TROUBLE IN ASIA

In Asia, Japan's power was growing. It invaded China in 1937. This started a bitter campaign that would leave millions dead. Japan wanted to control East Asia and the Pacific. They signed agreements with Germany and Italy. The three countries promised to help each other out.

THE ROAD TO WAR

Hitler's armies marched into Austria in March 1938. Austria was now part of Germany. Next on Hitler's list of land to take over was the western part of Czechoslovakia, where many Germans lived. British and French leaders met with Hitler in Munich. They agreed to let him take the area. They thought this would prevent war, but they were wrong.

■ Prime Minister Chamberlain returned to London in triumph after signing the Munich Agreement.

After Munich, Prime Minister Neville Chamberlain spoke to the British people. He said: "For the second time in our history, a British prime minister has returned from Germany bringing peace with honour. I believe it is peace for our time."

Another politician, Winston Churchill, criticized the agreement. He said: "You were given the choice between war and dishonour. You chose dishonour, and you will have war."

Who Took Sides in the War?

It became clear that Hitler was thinking about invading Poland. British and French leaders said that they would help Poland if it was attacked. But Hitler wasn't too worried. He signed a secret agreement with the Soviet Union. It was a promise between the two countries not to go to war with each other. On September 1, 1939, Germany invaded Poland.

LINING UP

Within days, the United Kingdom and France declared war on Germany. Many countries decided to stay **neutral** rather than taking sides. But neutrality didn't always save them from invasion. After eight months with little fighting, the Germans attacked. They took over Norway, Denmark, Luxembourg, Belgium, the Netherlands, and France.

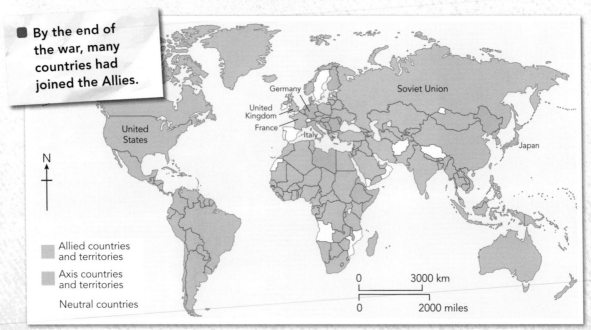

By the end of the war, many countries had joined the Allies.

Germany
United Kingdom
France
Italy
United States
Soviet Union
Japan

N

Allied countries and territories

Axis countries and territories

Neutral countries

0   3000 km

0   2000 miles

The two sides became known as the "Axis" and the "Allies." Germany, Italy, and Japan made up the Axis. They were later joined by other Eastern European countries. After France fell, the main Allies were the United Kingdom and China. They were joined by the Soviet Union in June 1941.

THE UNITED STATES

The United States was determined to stay out of another bloody European war. However, President Franklin D. Roosevelt was sympathetic to the Allies. He helped his country provide them with weapons and other supplies. Then, on December 7, 1941, the Japanese attacked Hawaii. Their target was the naval base at Pearl Harbor. The United States entered the war the next day.

■ Both sides used **propaganda** to affect public opinion.

HISTORY UNLOCKED

Roosevelt gave a speech on December 8, asking Congress to declare war. He said: "There is no blinking at the fact that our people, our territory, and our interests are in grave danger."

What Deadly Weapons Were Used?

Weapons in WWII ranged from traditional to cutting-edge. During the war, engineers raced to come up with bigger and better weapons. Tiny improvements, such as making a plane a bit faster, could make a huge difference. Factories worked around the clock to produce vehicles, weapons, and ammunition. Keeping troops supplied was a huge job.

GUNS AND ARTILLERY

Most foot soldiers carried weapons such as pistols, rifles, and grenades. These weapons had been around since the last war, but the newer models were more efficient and reliable. Armies also depended on **artillery**. These large guns shot explosive shells over long distances. They could be used to destroy enemy defenses before an attack.

With so many men away fighting, women were hired to produce weapons.

TANK WARFARE

Tanks made their first appearance in World War I. By the 1930s, they had improved enormously. They played a much larger role in WWII. Tanks had heavy, powerful guns that could inflict a lot of damage. Their caterpillar tracks let them be driven almost anywhere.

American soldiers used a new weapon, the bazooka, against tanks. This portable rocket launcher could be used by a single soldier. It fired small explosive rockets. They could penetrate through armor about 5 inches (12 centimeters) thick.

FATAL FACTS

Tanks could be death traps. The M4 Sherman tank was one of the main types used during the war, but it had a reputation for catching fire after taking a hit. It was even worse when the fire ignited the ammunition stored inside. Whole crews could be killed this way.

Turret can rotate 360 degrees to find targets

Crew of 5 entered through the hatch

The German Tiger II tank combined heavy armor with a powerful gun.

Gun fires 22-pound (10-kg) shells

Tough caterpillar tracks for traveling over wet or rough ground

Thick, sloping armor to protect the tank from enemy fire

FIGHTING SHIPS

The war was fought at sea as well as on land. Both sides wanted to control the main shipping routes. If they could cut off the enemy's supply lines, it gave them an advantage. Navies used enormous battleships, which were heavily armed. They could hit targets accurately from almost 20 miles (32 kilometers) away. Destroyers were smaller and more nimble. They used **torpedoes** and guns against other ships.

HIDDEN BENEATH THE WAVES

Submarines could launch surprise attacks by approaching from below. The Germans used more submarines than any other country, but nearly 800 of them were sunk. Often the whole crew would be killed. The German submarine service lost 68 percent of its sailors. About 28,000 were killed.

German submarines sank about 3,000 Allied ships during the war.

AIRCRAFT CARRIERS

Aircraft carriers let navies launch bombing raids almost anywhere in the world. Planes could take off, land, refuel, and take off again. Aircraft carriers had an advantage over battleships. The planes they launched had greater range than naval guns. They could hit targets more accurately.

Planes on aircraft carriers could fold up their wings to save space.

The United States and Japan were fighting for control of the Pacific Ocean. Their aircraft carriers clashed in several huge battles. The biggest was the Battle of Leyte Gulf in 1944. Australian forces joined the United States to inflict huge losses on the Japanese.

BATTLE OF LEYTE GULF BY THE NUMBERS

		Allied forces	Japanese forces
Aircraft carriers		8	1
Smaller carriers		26	3
Battleships		12	9
Cruisers		24	20
Destroyers		166	35
Airplanes		1,500	300

WARPLANES

Airplanes were a key weapon during the war. Some flew from aircraft carriers. Others operated from airfields on land. Planes could take photos of enemy positions. Fighter planes, such as the British Spitfire, shot down enemy planes. Bombers dropped explosives on troops, factories, and ports.

■ The Hawker Hurricane fighter was used to attack bombers approaching Britain.

BOMBING RAIDS

Both sides launched bombing raids on enemy cities. The biggest type of bomb weighed 11 tons (10,000 kg) and could go through thick concrete. **Incendiary bombs** were designed to start fires. In March 1945, a raid dropped 500,000 incendiary bombs on Toyko. About 100,000 people died.

HISTORY UNLOCKED

French reporter Robert Guillain wrote this after witnessing the **firebombing** of Tokyo.

"As they fell, cylinders scattered a kind of flaming dew that skittered along the roofs, setting fire to everything it splashed and spreading a wash of dancing flames everywhere."

LONG-RANGE MISSILES

During the war, the Germans developed jet-powered missiles. The first of these, the V-1, could fly up to 93 miles (150 km). It could be launched from France and still hit London. The next version, the V-2, was bigger and deadlier. In the United Kingdom, these weapons killed about 6,000 people. The bombs dropped by aircraft killed many more: about 43,000.

ATOMIC WEAPONS

Before the war, scientists had learned how to split atoms. Now each side raced to turn this knowledge into powerful atomic weapons. The U.S. carried out the first successful test in July 1945. They dropped two bombs on Japan the following month. The bombs killed hundreds of thousands of people.

The V-2 missile was the basis for the space rockets that were developed after the war.

EXPLOSIVE POWER OF WEAPONS COMPARED TO TONS OF TNT

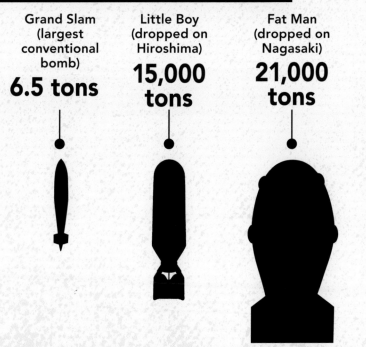

Grand Slam (largest conventional bomb)

6.5 tons

Little Boy (dropped on Hiroshima)

15,000 tons

Fat Man (dropped on Nagasaki)

21,000 tons

Where Was the War Fought?

In the spring of 1940, German troops rolled through western Europe. They pushed the Allied troops back to the French coast. About 338,000 soldiers were evacuated from Dunkirk in early June. After that, there was little fighting in Western Europe until 1944. Instead, the focus of the war shifted south and east.

ITALY AND THE BALKANS

In October 1940, Italy invaded Greece, but was soon beaten back. Germany then invaded Yugoslavia before moving on to Greece. Allied forces didn't invade southern Europe until July 1943. They landed in Sicily and slowly pushed north. Mussolini was removed from power, and Italy surrendered in September.

■ Allied bombers pounded German positions in Italy.

HISTORY UNLOCKED

One British soldier fighting in Italy saw his friend die. He wrote this in his diary.

"With a foot blown off, he neither cried nor passed out for quite a while. One must be forced to the conclusion that he knew how he was going to take it."

INVADING THE SOVIET UNION

Hitler's agreement with the Soviet Union didn't last long. In June 1941, the German army launched a surprise attack. Hitler thought he could take the country quickly, but he was wrong. After reaching Moscow, his army was pushed back. The freezing winter and lack of supplies killed many soldiers. The battle dragged on for years. The invading army killed civilians as well as enemy troops.

FATAL FACTS

For 872 days, the Soviet city of Leningrad was surrounded by the German army. Supplies were cut off, and people began to starve. The cold winters also killed many people. About one million Soviet civilians and soldiers died during the **siege**.

This statue honors the people who defended Leningrad (now called St Petersburg).

THE WAR IN THE PACIFIC

At first, the only fighting in Asia was in China. But Japan wanted to rule the entire Pacific region. Japanese forces attacked the US naval base at Pearl Harbor on December 7, 1941. The same day, they also attacked other Allied territories. Hong Kong, Malaya (now called Malaysia), and the Philippines were all invaded. The well-trained Japanese army made huge gains at first. The fighting in Southeast Asia and the Pacific was incredibly fierce.

HISTORY UNLOCKED

A U.S. Air Force pilot wrote this description of a bombing raid over the Pacific islands of Palau.

"About this time a black Zeke appeared on our left out of machine gun range. He flew there for several minutes without attempting to attack. Then the stuff hit the fan! We were attacked from all directions by Tojos and Zekes."

("Tojo" and "Zeke" were slang terms for types of Japanese fighter planes.)

■ The attack on Pearl Harbor left more than 2,400 Americans dead.

NAVAL BATTLES

Two major naval battles helped the Allies gain an edge. The Battle of the Coral Sea took place in May 1942. The U.S. Navy defeated the Japanese. This blocked their path to Australia. The next month, the U.S. Navy won the Battle of Midway. More than 3,000 Japanese troops were killed. Four of their aircraft carriers were sunk.

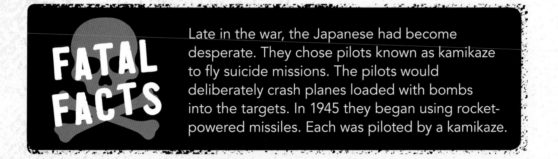

FATAL FACTS

Late in the war, the Japanese had become desperate. They chose pilots known as kamikaze to fly suicide missions. The pilots would deliberately crash planes loaded with bombs into the targets. In 1945 they began using rocket-powered missiles. Each was piloted by a kamikaze.

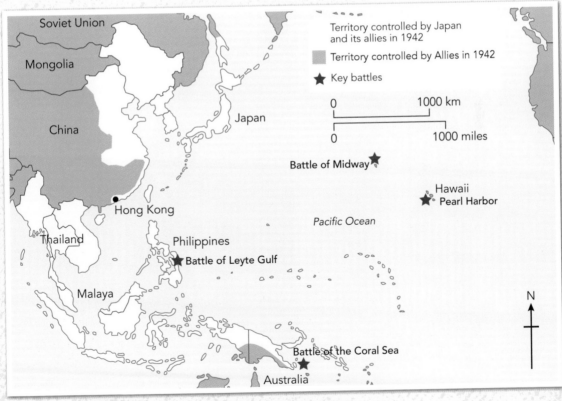

This map shows some of the main battles in the Pacific region.

AFRICA AND THE MIDDLE EAST

The Allies needed to keep control of the Suez Canal in Egypt. They used it to send supplies by sea from Europe to India and elsewhere in Asia. But British troops in Egypt were attacked by the Italians. The British won several battles. Then the Germans arrived to help the Italians. Under the command of Erwin Rommel, they pushed the British back into Egypt.

In October 1942, the two sides met in a huge tank battle at el-Alamein. Allied ships in the Mediterranean had kept supplies from reaching the Axis forces. The Allies had more tanks, more equipment, and more men. They won a decisive victory. About 14,000 soldiers on both sides were killed. Another 24,000 were wounded. 35,000 were taken prisoner.

Newspapers reported on the fighting in North Africa.

Bernard Montgomery

Bernard Montgomery was a British general. His men affectionately called him "Monty." After taking part in the Dunkirk evacuation, he commanded British troops in North Africa. He later helped lead the Allied armies into France.

OTHER BATTLES

Italian forces had taken control of East Africa. In 1941, they were defeated by the British. There was also fighting in the Middle East. Most of this region had been under the control of European countries. Some of it still was. Some people supported the Axis, and others supported the Allies. There was bloody fighting in Iraq, Iran, Syria, Lebanon, and Palestine.

HISTORY UNLOCKED

Before el-Alamein, the British army had started using American-built Sherman tanks. These tanks were tougher and more powerful than the German tanks at the time. They carried a crew of five and had armor 4 inches (11 cm) thick.

THE BATTLE OF THE ATLANTIC

Getting supplies — such as food, weapons, troops, and raw materials — was crucial. Cutting off an enemy's supplies could really hurt them. Many of these supplies were sent by ship. The north Atlantic Ocean became a battleground. Both sides tried to keep the other's ships from getting through.

At first, British and French ships had the advantage. They were able to **blockade** Germany. But after France fell to the Nazis, the British navy struggled to cope. Ships traveled in **convoys** for protection. Military ships would escort groups of 20 to 60 commercial vessels. They would try to fight off attackers.

This American oil tanker was one of many merchant ships sunk by the enemy.

WOLF PACKS

Destroyers and other warships attacked convoys. But German **U-boats** were the biggest threat to shipping. They used a tactic called the "wolf pack." The U-boats would patrol in a long line. Once a convoy was spotted, they would converge on it. Even if some were chased or sunk by the convoy's escorts, others could still attack.

CRACKING THE CODE

The German U-boats kept in touch by radio. They used a machine called Enigma to encode their messages. They thought that the code was unbreakable, but the British managed to crack it. More importantly, they kept their success a secret. They used intercepted messages to find and attack wolf packs.

The Enigma used a combination of keys and rotors to encode messages.

FATAL FACTS

In September 1941, a convoy of 64 merchant ships sailed from Canada to England. They were escorted by four navy ships. A wolf pack of 14 U-boats was waiting near Greenland. They sank 16 of the ships. Only about 300 sailors were killed, but important supplies were lost.

THE BATTLE OF THE ATLANTIC BY THE NUMBERS

750
German U-boats took part, of which

510
were sunk

27,000
German U-boat sailors took part, of whom

18,000
were killed

2,200
Allied ships sunk

at least
30,000
Allied merchant seamen killed

at least
30,000
Allied sailors killed

Why Did So Many Civilians Die?

Everyone in the fighting nations was affected by the war. A country had to throw everything into its war effort. Factories were converted to produce weapons and uniforms. Fuel was saved for use by the armed forces. Naval blockades often kept goods and raw materials from arriving. The armed forces took priority, so people at home often had to do without.

MINISTRY **MF** OF FOOD

RATION BOOK
1944-45

Surname..

Other Names...

Address...
(as on Identity Card)
....

Date of birth (Day)............... (Month)...............

NATIONAL
REGISTRATION
NUMBER

FOOD OFFICE CODE No.

N.

M.F.

8.17

IF FOUND RETURN TO ANY FOOD OFFICE

HISTORY UNLOCKED

In the United Kingdom, every person was issued a **ration** book. It had coupons for foods such as eggs, sugar, and meat. When you bought food at a shop, you gave the shopkeeper some of your coupons. This way, food was shared equally. Clothes and fuel were also rationed.

THE BLITZ

Airplanes helped armies launch attacks from far away. This meant that civilians far from the front lines became targets. Starting in September 1940, German planes began dropping bombs on civilian targets in the United Kingdom. This "Blitz" lasted for eight months. About 43,000 people were killed.

Fire crews in London raced to put out fires caused by bombs.

ALLIED BOMBING RAIDS

The Allies fought back with bombing raids in Axis territory. German cities such as Hamburg, Cologne, and Düsseldorf were heavily bombed. These raids targeted factories and docks as well as residential areas. The U.S. Air Force firebombed Japanese cities, killing hundreds of thousands. Even civilians in occupied France were not safe. Many were killed as Allied bombers tried to destroy factories.

FATAL FACTS

In February 1945, Allied planes bombed Dresden, Germany. The raid lasted for three days. On the first night, 800 airplanes dropped 2,700 tons (2,450 tonnes) of bombs. Incendiary bombs started fires. The raid killed about 25,000 people.

OCCUPIED TERRITORIES

Millions of people lived in territories that were occupied by enemy forces. They tried to keep going as normal. Life could be very hard, though. In Europe, the Nazis controlled many aspects of life. Civilians could be forced to work for the Nazis. Many were killed or sent to **concentration camps**.

The Japanese occupied large parts of China and southeast Asia. In many places, they imposed **martial law**. People who didn't cooperate could be arrested, tortured, and even executed.

RESISTANCE

Secret **resistance** groups sprang up in these areas. They tried to disrupt the enemy's operations. Resistance fighters blew up railroads and damaged factories. They passed information to Allied forces. It was very dangerous, and many were caught and killed.

Hannie Schaft

Hannie Schaft was a Dutch law student. When the Nazis occupied the Netherlands, she refused to sign an oath of loyalty. She joined a resistance group. They worked to hide Jewish people and gather information. In 1945, she was captured and executed.

■ For most of the war, the Nazi flag flew over much of Europe.

INTERNMENT CAMPS

Even in free territories, civilians could be detained. Citizens of other nations were seen as a threat. In the United States, 120,000 Japanese Americans were sent to **internment camps**. They stayed there, under guard, for the rest of the war. Thousands of Germans and Italians were interned in the United Kingdom.

FATAL FACTS

Many of the people interned in the United Kingdom were sent to camps in Canada. A passenger ship on its way to Canada was was torpedoed by a German U-boat in 1940. About 800 people were killed. Many of them were **internees**.

Japanese Americans were forced to leave their homes.

LIVING IN A WAR ZONE

When troops and tanks rolled across the land, they left chaos in their wake. They destroyed buildings and took food and other supplies. Fierce battles were fought in villages, towns, and cities. In August 1942, the German army attacked Stalingrad. Soviet leaders didn't let civilians leave. They thought their army would fight harder in order to protect civilians.

The battle raged for months, and many civilians were caught up in it. Buildings were reduced to rubble as the fighting went on. About 40,000 civilians were killed. Between 1 and 2 million soldiers were killed, wounded, or captured.

■ The battle of Stalingrad lasted five months before the Germans surrendered.

REFUGEES

No one wanted to be caught in the crossfire. Others knew they would be persecuted by the invaders. Huge numbers of people left their homes, fleeing the fighting. Historians estimate that about 60 million people became **refugees** during the war. Finding food and shelter was a constant struggle.

SCORCHED EARTH

Retreating troops didn't want to leave anything that could be useful to the enemy. They often burned crops and destroyed bridges. This "scorched earth" policy made life very hard for locals. Homes were destroyed, and many people were killed. Japanese actions in China were called the "Three Alls Policy." This meant "kill all, burn all, loot all."

FATAL FACTS

Hunger probably killed more people during the war than anything else. Historians think that 20 million people starved to death. In occupied Greece, the Axis armies took food for their own use. Blockades kept supplies from arriving. Over the winter of 1941-42, about 100,000 Greeks died of starvation.

■ Starving Berliners searched for food in garbage dumps.

What War Crimes Were Committed?

The war saw terrible cruelty and suffering. Before World War II, it was accepted that this was just part of war. But the mistreatment and killing of civilians and prisoners horrified the world. Both sides had committed acts that can be considered **war crimes**. These actions ranged from mistreatment of prisoners of war (POWs) to civilian massacres and **genocide**.

PRISONERS OF WAR

The Geneva Convention was drawn up in 1929. It said that prisoners of war must be treated humanely. Their captors had to let neutral observers visit prison camps. France, Germany, the United Kingdom and the U.S. were bound by this agreement. Japan and the Soviet Union had signed it but never officially ratified it, so they were not.

■ POW camps were often crowded, but in some the prisoners were well cared for.

Millions of soldiers were taken prisoner during the war. Germany treated British, French, and American POWs fairly well. However, they treated Soviet and Polish POWs much more harshly. More than 3 million Soviet POWs died in German captivity. Many starved to death. The Soviets responded by sending hundreds of thousands of German POWs to labor camps. Most of them died.

Airey Neave

Airey Neave was a British officer captured in France in 1940. After escaping from a POW camp, he was sent to the high-security prison at Colditz. He was the first British soldier to escape from Colditz.

HISTORY UNLOCKED

Food was sometimes in short supply in POW camps. The Red Cross in the United Kingdom, Canada, and the U.S. sent more than 60 million packages to inmates. They contained food such as butter, chocolate, and powdered milk.

POWS IN ASIA

POWs held by the Japanese often received very harsh treatment. Captured Allied soldiers were beaten and forced to work as slave labor. They had little food or medical care. Tens of thousands of them died.

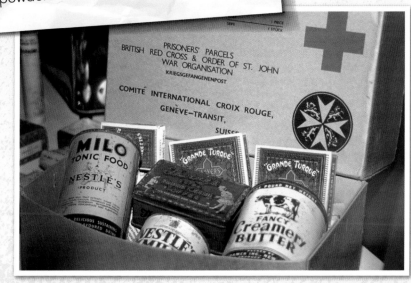

TARGETING CIVILIANS

In World War II, civilians were in the firing line. Both sides killed people who were seen as expendable. Some military leaders thought targeting civilians would hurt morale. Others thought that their enemies were inferior and deserved to die. Bombs killed hundreds of thousands. There were also other ways of targeting civilians.

FORCED LABOR

In occupied Poland, all men were forced to do unpaid labor. They worked in factories, built railroads, and dug tunnels. Working conditions were often dangerous. Many sites were targeted by Allied bombers. In Asia, millions of Chinese civilians were forced to work for the Japanese.

■ The Japanese used Chinese workers to help re-open an important road.

MASSACRES

Some of the most horrifying events were massacres. Hundreds or even thousands of people would be killed in one brutal attack. In 1937, Japanese troops took control of Nanjing, China. They rampaged through the streets. Between 100,000 and 300,000 civilians were killed. In Russia, Soviet soldiers took more than 4,400 Polish officers into the Katyn forest and executed them.

FATAL FACTS

The resistance was causing trouble in occupied France. The Nazis wanted revenge. They rounded up everyone in the village of Oradour-sur-Glane. They locked them in buildings, then set them on fire. 190 men, 245 women, and 207 children died. Only 10 survived.

■ Nazi troops massacred the people of the Czech village of Lidice. It was revenge for the assassination of a high-ranking Nazi, even though the villagers had nothing to do with it.

THE HOLOCAUST

Hitler and the Nazis hated the Jewish people. They thought that Jewish people were responsible for Germany's problems. Even before the war, Jewish people in Germany were persecuted. Once the war started, the Nazis took it further. They began to make plans for getting rid of all of the Jewish people in Europe. They called this the "Final Solution."

Wherever the German army went, they rounded up Jewish people. Some were killed right away, and some were sent to live in crowded **ghettos**. Others were used as slave labor. They were given little food and worked until they collapsed.

■ **These Jewish women are being led into the woods to be shot.**

CONCENTRATION CAMPS

Hitler sent special troops to kill Jewish people in occupied territories. These groups probably killed about 1 million people. However, it wasn't efficient enough for the Nazis. They started sending Jewish people to concentration camps, such as Auschwitz. Men, women, and children would be forced onto crowded freight trains. Once they arrived, some would be selected to work as slaves. Others were sent directly to gas chambers, where they were killed with poison gas. Their bodies were then burned.

OTHER VICTIMS

Jewish people were the main victims, but other groups suffered too. Polish and Romani people died in concentration camps. So did thousands of homosexuals and disabled people. The Nazis also targeted those with political ideas that they didn't like. Millions of people were killed.

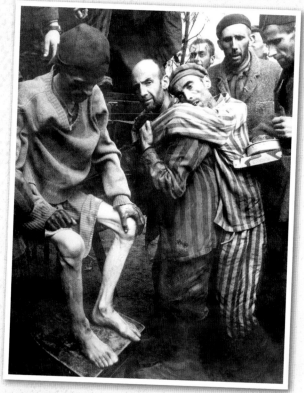

Many inmates in concentration camps starved to death.

COUNTRIES THAT LOST MOST OF THEIR JEWISH POPULATION DURING THE HOLOCAUST

Country	Percentage
Hungary	69%
Netherlands	71%
Latvia	78%
Lithuania	85%
Greece	86%
Poland	90%

How Did the War End?

The Axis powers made huge gains early in the war. But when the United States entered the war, it was a big boost to the Allies. They provided much-needed troops and equipment. In late 1942, after some key Allied victories, the tide began to turn. Italy surrendered in September 1943.

PROBLEMS FOR THE AXIS

The Germans were running low on men and equipment. Blockades kept food and raw materials from getting through. Factories were hit by Allied bombing raids. Even worse, the invasion of the Soviet Union had gone horribly wrong. German troops were being pushed back. In the Pacific, Japan didn't have the resources to keep control of the lands they had captured. The U.S. Navy had destroyed much of their fleet.

■ Victory by U.S. troops in the Battle of Leyte in 1944 was the first step toward re-taking the Philippines.

D-DAY

Bombing raids had caused real damage in occupied Europe. Now the Allies thought the time was right for an invasion. On June 6, 1944, Allied soldiers landed in northern France. About 7,000 ships set sail from England. They landed 133,000 soldiers on the beaches.

The Germans fought back, but it was the beginning of the end. By the end of June, 850,000 Allied soldiers and 150,000 vehicles had arrived in France. In the east, Soviet troops were making gains. Hitler's days were numbered.

Dwight D. Eisenhower

Dwight D. Eisenhower was an American general. He led U.S. troops in North Africa and Italy. He then planned and supervised the D-Day invasion. He was elected President in 1952.

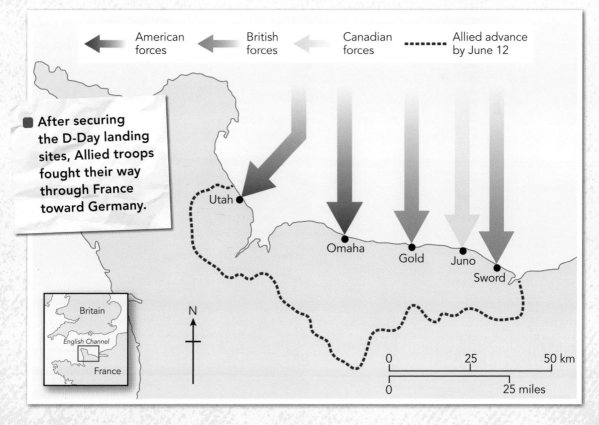

After securing the D-Day landing sites, Allied troops fought their way through France toward Germany.

American forces

British forces

Canadian forces

Allied advance by June 12

Utah

Omaha

Gold

Juno

Sword

Britain

English Channel

France

N

0   25   50 km

0   25 miles

39

THE FALL OF BERLIN

By late 1944, Allied armies were closing in on Germany. Hitler launched one last, desperate attack in Belgium in December. The Allies managed to push back the German troops. Soviet soldiers reached Berlin in April. They pounded it with shells and fought their way in. On April 30, Hitler committed suicide. His deputies surrendered, and on May 8, the war in Europe was over.

Victorious Soviet soldiers raised their flag over Berlin.

WAR IN THE PACIFIC

However, fighting in the Pacific still raged. The Japanese armed forces had been weakened. American bombers destroyed towns and industrial sites. Ground troops slowly pushed their way forward. About 20,000 Japanese soldiers died defending the island of Iwo Jima. Some killed themselves rather than surrender.

ENDING THE WAR

The Allies did not want to have to invade Japan. Previous battles had cost many lives on both sides. The Japanese had shown that they would not give up, but would keep fighting. However, the United States had a powerful new weapon: atomic bombs. Using them against Japan would kill hundreds of thousands of civilians. But they might end the war, preventing a long and bloody invasion. U.S. President Harry Truman decided to use them. The cities of Hiroshima and Nagasaki were bombed in August. A week later, Japan surrendered.

More than half the buildings in Hiroshima were destroyed in the bombing.

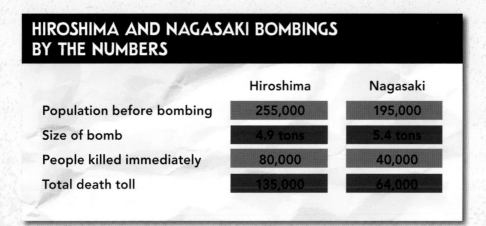

HIROSHIMA AND NAGASAKI BOMBINGS BY THE NUMBERS

	Hiroshima	Nagasaki
Population before bombing	255,000	195,000
Size of bomb	4.9 tons	5.4 tons
People killed immediately	80,000	40,000
Total death toll	135,000	64,000

What Were the Effects of the War?

The war was over, but the world was in chaos. Tens of millions of people had died. Just as many were now refugees, trying to find a way home. Cities and towns had been reduced to rubble. Food was scarce. In many places, there was no real authority. Violence and looting were common.

After the war, people in occupied countries who had cooperated with the Nazis were publicly shamed.

JUSTICE FOR THE VICTIMS

Many people wanted revenge for what had happened. The Holocaust and other acts were classified as war crimes. Hundreds of German and Japanese leaders and soldiers were tried and executed. A few Allied soldiers were also tried for committing war crimes.

Top Nazis such as Hermann Goering (center) were tried and sentenced to death.

PREVENTING ANOTHER WAR

Everyone agreed that another world war must never happen. World leaders founded the United Nations in October 1945. This organization tries to maintain peace and settle disputes between nations. They have even sent peacekeeping troops to conflict areas.

A NEW WORLD ORDER

The United States and the Soviet Union were now the world's main superpowers. They had been allies, but they were radically different. The US was based on **capitalism** and democracy. The Soviet Union was **communist**. Their clash of ideals shaped the next few decades.

Timeline

1933–1938

January 30, 1933	Adolf Hitler becomes Chancellor of Germany.
July 7, 1937	Japan invades China.
March 13, 1938	Germany takes control of Austria.
September 29, 1938	Germany, France, Italy, and the United Kingdom sign the Munich Agreement.

1939

August 23	Germany and the Soviet Union sign a secret agreement not to go to war.
September 1	Germany invades Poland.
September 3	France and the United Kingdom declare war on Germany.

1940

April 9	Germany invades Denmark and Norway.
May 10	Germany invades Belgium, the Netherlands, and Luxembourg. Winston Churchill becomes prime minister of the United Kingdom.
May 26–June 3	British and French troops are evacuated from Dunkirk, France.
June 22	France and Germany sign an armistice.
July–October	Germany conducts bombing raids on military and industrial targets in the United Kingdom.

1941

Sept 1940–May 1941	German bombers attack civilian targets in Britain.
22 June 22	Germany invades the Soviet Union.
September 8	Leningrad is cut off by the German army and a siege begins.
December 7	Japan attacks the U.S. naval base at Pearl Harbor, Hawaii.
December 8	The U.S. and United Kingdom declare war on Japan.

1942

May 4–8	The Battle of the Coral Sea repels a Japanese invasion.
June 6	The Battle of Midway ends in a U.S. victory over Japan.
November 6	The Allies win the Battle of el-Alamein in North Africa.

1943

January 31	The Battle of Stalingrad ends with a German surrender.
September 8	Italy surrenders and leaves the war.

1944

January 27	The siege of Leningrad finally ends.
June 6	D-Day: Allied troops invade northern France.
August 25	Paris is liberated from German control.
October 20	U.S. troops invade the Philippines.
October 23–26	The Battle of Leyte Gulf ends with an Allied victory.
December 16	The Battle of the Bulge (Germany's last major offensive) begins.

1945

February 13–15	Allied planes firebomb Dresden, Germany.
March 9–10	The U.S. firebombs Tokyo.
April 22	Soviet troops enter Berlin.
April 30	Hitler commits suicide.
May 8	Germany surrenders, and the war in Europe is over.
August 6	The U.S. drops an atomic bomb on Hiroshima, Japan.
August 9	A second atomic bomb is dropped on the Japanese city of Nagasaki.
August 15	Japan surrenders and the war ends.
October 24	The United Nations organization begins operation.

GLOSSARY

ammunition (am-yuh-NI-shuhn)—bullets and other objects that can be fired from weapons

artillery (ar-TI-luhr-ee)—cannons and other large guns used during battles

atomic bomb (uh-TOM-ik BOM)—a powerful bomb that explodes with great force and leaves behind dangerous radiation

blockade (blok-AYD)—a closing off of an area to keep people or supplies from going in or out

capitalism (CAP-it-ul-i-zuhm)—economic system that allows people to create businesses and own as much property as they can afford

chancellor (CHAN-suh-luhr)—a title for the leader of a country

civilian (si-VIL-yuhn)—a person who is not in the military

communism (KAHM-yuh-ni-zuhm)—a way of organizing a country so that all the land, houses, and factories belong to the government, and the profits are shared by all

compensation (com-pen-SAY-shun)—money paid in recognition of loss or suffering

concentration camp (kahn-suhn-TRAY-shuhn KAMP)—a prison camp where thousands of inmates are held under harsh conditions

convoy (KAHN-voy)—a protective escort of ships or boats

democracy (di-MAH-kruh-see)—a form of government in which the citizens can choose their leaders

depression (di-PRE-shuhn)—a period during which business, jobs, and stock values stay low

dictator (DIK-tay-tuhr)—someone who has complete control of a country

fascism (FASH-i-zuhm)—right-wing form of government with extreme nationalistic ideals

firebomb (FYR BAHM)—to target with incendiary bombs

genocide (JEN-oh-side)—to destroy a race of people on purpose

ghetto (GET-oh)—a poor neighborhood in a city where people of the same race live

incendiary bomb (in-SEND-ee-air-ee BAHM)—bomb that is filled with flammable material, designed to start fires

inflation (in-FLAY-shuhn)—an increase in prices

internee (in-tuhr-NEE)—person detained in an internment camp

internment camp (in-TERN-ment KAMP)—place where citizens are detained because they are seen to be a danger during war

martial law (MAR-shul LAW)—control of a people by the government's military, instead of by civilian forces, often during an emergency

neutral (NOO-truhl)—not taking any side in a war

propaganda (PROP-uh-GAN-duh)—information spread to try to influence the thinking of people

primary source (PRYE-mair-ee SORSS)—source from someone who experienced an event firsthand

ration (RASH-uhn)—limit on an item intented to ensure that it doesn't run out

refugee (ref-yuh-JEE)—a person forced to flee his or her home because of natural disaster or war

resistance (ri-ZISS-tuhnss)—secret organization resisting authority in an occupied country

siege (SEEJ)—an attack designed to surround a place and cut it off from supplies or help

tactic (TAK-tik)—a plan for fighting a battle

torpedo (tor-PEE-doh)—an underwater missile

U-boat (YOU BOTE)—a German submarine

war crime (WAR KRYM)—act that violates the accepted international rules of war

READ MORE

Books

Biskup, Agnieszka. *D-Day*. 24-Hour History. Chicago: Raintree, 2015.

Marriott, Emma. *Did Anything Good Come Out of World War II?* Innovation Through Adversity. New York: Rosen Publishing, 2016.

Servin, Morgan. *World War II Close Up*. The War Chronicles. New York: Rosen Publishing, 2016.

Stein, R. Conrad. *World War II in the Pacific: From Pearl Harbor to Nagasaki*. The United States at War. New York: Enslow Publishing, 2011.

Throp, Claire. *Resisting the Nazis*. Heroes of World War II. Chicago: Raintree, 2016.

Internet Sites

FactHound offers a safe, fun way to find Internet sites related to this book. All of the sites on FactHound have been researched by our staff.

Here's all you do:

Visit *www.facthound.com*

Type in this code: 9781484841651

Places to Visit

Museum of Science and Industry
5700 S. Lake Shore Drive
Chicago, IL 60637
https://www.msichicago.org

National Museum of American History
Constitution Avenue, NW
Washington, D.C. 20001
http://americanhistory.si.edu

National World War II Memorial
900 Ohio Drive SW
Washington, D.C. 20024
https://www.nps.gov/wwii/index.htm

Critical Thinking Questions

Which parts of this book did you find the most interesting? What subjects would you like to know more about?

How did the end of World War I set the stage for World War II?

Describe how life for civilians in occupied territories was different from life for civilians away from the front lines. Support your answer using information from at least two other texts or valid Internet sources.

In what ways were civilians targeted? Why were both sides willing to target civilians? Support your answer using information from at least two other texts or valid Internet resources.

INDEX